TO KISS WHAT CANNOT BE KISSED...

TO KISS WHAT CANNOT BE KISSED...

Love songs from the canyon

NANCY NEITHERCUT

ISBN-13: 9781545419557
ISBN-10: 1545419558

CHAPTERS...

DEAR READERS,

I can only express what it's like after this profound shift in perspective, knowing that this is the dream as well. Knowing that it can't be shared or kissed with words, and that there is no one with whom to share.

But we can sit together on this bench under the tall Pines on the edge of the cliffs of this shore-less ocean, and gaze out together at the featureless sea, and marvel at the imaginary line where the sky kisses its reflection in blue.

We can share the amazement and the unbearable unspeakable beauty of life just as it is. The stunning magical and mysterious nature of life living itself, touching itself, kissing itself through us.

We can feel the breath of sunset as it whispers in our delicate tender hearts. And marvel that we can see our own reflections in each other's beautiful beautiful eyes.

Songs flow like the wind creating light and shadow, and the river of our hearts swells and soars touching all and everything with a love that cannot be caught.

I was a seeker because of the pain because of the giant hole in my heart, and I found out that I existed only as this most beautiful sublime tender achy breaky heart

All that I feared so much, the impermanence, the deep deep feeling, the longing to feel all that love I was terrified to lose... The heartbreak, the overwhelming longing for something which I knew not...
Becomes most beautiful as it is truly no longer mine...

My heart unraveled the strings play silently a symphony of one of two of many of none, of love and love lost, of infinite tapestries ever blooming simultaneously wilting....

It was the tender delicate sensitive wetness of my eyes that I feared, that all that crying would kill me for sure

But it's like the tears were razors as they eviscerated me of any belief of substance, of permanency, of any place to land, anything to hold, and my fingers dissolved in tears of laughter joy sorrow, of awe.

This nu-utterable ferocious terrifying utterly naked emptiness filled every secret pore of my being, eviscerated me ravished me whole and ripped me inside out, pulled my heart out so that it's very beating crushed me.

Under that skin I so longed to lose there was not even nothing. No one to be lost or found, confused or clear, awakened or asleep. So I found that pile of clothes by the bed and those old comfortable dancing shoes and waltzed into the dream as life kisses itself through my lips. As life sings the ultimate love song of this life... this precious life... this splendid dream lush and rich beyond measure.

Sparkling aliveness breathes through me as me and my heart weeps at this intimate beauty this infinite spaciousness wrapped embraced in the kiss of wind, the sigh of star-light, the sailing soaring utter nakedness of life unowned.

Awakening is the deepest Intimacy as your own love has ravished you skinned you alive and ripped out your heart your love and your life.

All that's left is the dance of one of two of none... streaming moving and standing utterly still without a ground or goal or place to be, singing vibrantly silently a mad passionate dance of you of me of we.

It is like love this beautiful homelessness. This feeling of soaring skinless as the wind. This vibrant rushing roaring sublime perfection breathing my heart song.

Life and love continue to sail across a vast ocean of tears as the sunset reflects its beautiful beautiful oranges and reds on my sky lined face...
Never Born never dying always born always dying

Always weeping

The longing to sing of this unbearable beauty, knowing it cannot be held or given away. To kiss what cannot be kissed... paints my imaginary lines in sky. As flowing light and wind and color slide through me as me. Shine and shadow merge into a river of song

and Oh!
How can I fold this wonder into a bird and send it to you?
How can I hold my beating heart as it flies into a million pieces of emptiness?

How can I show you your infinite intimate emptiness and your beautiful breathtaking fullness?

How can I show you that this precious life is not even yours?
How can I give you a sip of the nectar of this beautiful unknowingness?
How can I slide a moonbeam into a bottle and throw your lovelight across the sea of dreams
How can I touch you as you are none other than me, yet a Grand Canyon divides us...
This yearning to touch you to sing of this paints this emptiness with a longing that sings me, such ineffable infinite wonder!

It is the rhythm of life that we share the heartbeat of existence this wondrous love.

I cannot give you anything.
I cannot give you nothing.
Where would you put it?

It's not that I know more than you
There is a delicious unknowing and no longer a need to know, to grasp or capture life. There is a vacancy where someone to know would be, a sublime certitude with un-certitude.

I did not do or not do anything or nothing to have this happen. I have not achieved something or arrived somewhere. Awakening is truly an empty prize for no one.
It's like winning the lottery without buying a ticket, and you hold out your hands to gather the prize, but the gold falls through them. Everything is gold.

I have no instructions or counsel, as there is no right or wrong way to feel, to think, to believe, to act and no chooser of these things, and no separate things to choose from.

I have not escaped the dream of separation, I have not transcended my humanness.
This is not a special state of bliss or joy or peace or love, yet there is an indescribable sense of awe, a seamless ease, a sublime quiescence permeating saturating the dream of you of me of we.
Overwhelmingly wondrous that there is not even nothing here or there, and yet all and everything so vibrantly magnificently alive.

This is an entirely different way to experience the dream, but yes, it is the dream as well.

People ask me if I see as they do?
Do I see the way I used to see?

I look around and although I cannot go back, I can say, "well my eyes ears all my senses seem to be functioning the way they did before the shift, but the feeling tone is completely changed, as there is never the feeling of any separate things or separate moments. There's never the feeling that someone is doing life or that life is happening to a someone.

The thought stream has changed quite a lot as well. There's no more constant self judgment and self correction, as I no longer see imaginary characters, including myself, as the instigators or being responsible or indeed separate from thought feeling sensation or action.

It feels like a wondrous seamless timeless flow. It was always that way, it was just never noticed.
As it is always this way there is nothing that can be done to make it anew.

It's a constant streaming insight of the utter perfection of anything that seems to appear. There is no more hope or fear or need of other, better, more, or next.

It is the end of all belief in belief. It is the end of all belief in meaning or meaninglessness, of belief in truth or false, purpose or non purpose, freedom or non-freedom, or anyone to be free or bound.

It is the complete end of the belief that there is something to attain or someone to attain it.

It is life full on unabashedly naked. Feeling everything deeply yet somehow impersonally, like being in a movie, a passion play that writes and erases itself, and watching it at the same time.

The utter indescribable beauty of life doing itself.

But I am not a guru
Nor teacher
Just a lover of love...

Love,

Nancy

MOUNTAIN SONGS

....and every secret corner of your being unfolds into seamless sky...

and at higher altitudes you can finally see the plains rolling into vast forest... and your eyes are not separate from the seeing... the fabric of you has unraveled and been rewoven into a majestic endless measureless tapestry ...the edges have fallen away, yet every leaf is infused with its own brightness... perfect in its own right ...not a single dust mote out of place in this seamless flowing. You turn off the air conditioning and roll down the windows and bathe in sparkling mountain air. Your head is clear ...your eyes are cleansed of a lifetime of seeking the summit and you cry at the beauty ...of perfection ...a tiny petal falling ...the most scrumptious yellowy orange

and the day begins ...light fills the meadow ...streams through the laden grasses and many colored blossoms back-lit by these first rays ...hanging waving like lanterns in the soft breeze... small birds rise and dance in the shimmering ...a herd of does slowly cross ... grazing ...a hum of insects... chrysanthemum clouds bloom over the ridge ...they burst into a thousand petals and join again and block out the sun

Life simply happens and the brain uses shared learned words to write a story about it. The stories are beautiful... they include time ...and meaning... sumptuous ideas of a golden or terror-filed future and rated pictures of a past ...constantly viewing these images the story of you seems to exist in the middle

Yet it can be seen that that jester hat is empty ...it was merely the shiny musical bells that were hypnotizing... it can happen that the stories are no longer believed ...and there is living in the space before the stories are written and embracing the stories at the same time

the ripeness of life is always on... lush ...rich beyond measure ...far more than one could ever imagine or dream about ...the ordinary becomes the extraordinary and leaves you breathless and there is overwhelming wonder ...but there is never a wondering why ...like you drink water and it is wet

the simplicity of seeing feeling life unadorned ...instead of all these learned ideas of what it's supposed to be ...is utterly stunning ...when the cage of words becomes transparent the prison that was you becomes spectacular beyond measure, as there is no longer a longing to escape. How marvelous to be free of all that hope that the next step the next hour the next day will be better, and fear that it'll be worse.

And can you read all these words without trying to find their meaning? As no words or thoughts can ever touch what's going on. Any recipe for living is false. Any prescription for awakening is untrue. Already there is clear seeing. Only words and ideas have bamboozled your brain into believing that there's a separate you living a life called yours.

trying to mine the treasure the treasure is missed ...lost in a hole of darkness ...crying.. and my words are your words and you know this my heart is your heart... no heart escapes the inevitable loveliness the inevitable loneliness these insatiable tears for no one

all your ideas and thoughts about what life is about ...or supposed to be like, is like opening an umbrella under water... they merely seem to obscure the light... the iridescent wonder on the surface They don't keep you from getting wet...

all I can see is wings soaring and I turn to touch the shimmering ...and find my own heart smiling

long grasses waving on the meadow touched by long morning sun .infinite shades of greeny yellow oranges... dancing effortlessly for no one. no one knows what life is ...we sing our love songs and share the awe...and spin softly into each other's dream

drunk on her ideas of love she could no longer swallow ...lighting candles to the future she was left in darkness merely marking out her days until the great union she'd heard about would come. Till one day she saw through her reflection ...she poured her silhouette into a glass and drank deeply and realized that all she'd longed for were empty ideas... castles in the sky ...caught in a fortress she had built from dreams and all she had ever wanted was right here all along, and it was nothing at all

and purply clouds billow at night erasing the doldrums where you thought you lived ...it's a life without boredom this unpegged life... and the mountains dancing slowly. A night bird sings

away from the neon signs... chasing an idea of vastness ...darkness and misery snapping at your heels It's an endless race to freedom with no end in sight and without warning you fall into the sky you hear your name called and you fall into overwhelming silence

there is a sublime-ness in seamlesss ease ...a deafening all rightness ...there is a bitter-sweet beauty that no one can be touched ...that nothing can be touched... ever... and you reach out your hand ...and find yourself ...reaching out...

it's like light pouring itself softly from cup to cup. Then the cups disappear. Then the softly disappears. Then the pouring Disappears

And she holds up a treasure and says, 'oh my how beautiful' And I am simply a swoon of utter beauty. I am the sun flooding the meadow and delicate petals lantern'd flowing waving adrifting in seas of grasses and caressing the earth the sky the sound of winds in the pines from near and far sweeping down the mountain

Oh my this edgeless vast untraceable glowing lit from within from without without lines there is no one to be lost or found and I am their warmth and love and wonder as well as mine our breath our footfalls our shadows on the rippling ...the tender wetness of our eyes

Skinless splendid measureless unspeakable infinite flowing space filling overflowing emptiness without time nor non time this utter enormity of indescribable liquidity without end or source ....traceless light soaring sweeping through itself filling me emptying me I am the wind and life as they soar through me
Without others I simply cannot find a trace of a song to pretend to tether the wind. This is perhaps why we sing, those of us who have lost their imaginary piece of sky. Awe moves my pen as songs flow through me and write my imaginary lines.... always this silence singing Utter and complete the vastness expresses itself. Sings itself. Just. Like. This

Sun slides through the tips of the Pines and begins to bathe the clearing in Dawn... Electric needles shimmering vibrating outward... Sky trembling reaching inward.... vibrant alive-ness obscuring the imaginary lines between inside and out....

And do you remember when you got up every morning and wondered if this indeed would be the day? The day you would finally reach the summit of the mountain the peak the pinnacle of a lifetime of effort. A place always in the sun.. A place of utter and complete rest. A place where your journey would finally end. Because you had heard about this place, whispers in fairy tales from strangers and passersby, great and the small... writing singing of complete peace and perfection and the end of striving. And Oh my! How you have been striving! Desiring to stop desiring! Reaching to stop reaching! Seeking to stop seeking

And the roar of the mountain river and the winds soaring through the pines echoed your heart song and pierced you deeply. You were so tired of this endless path you had only glimpses of the top sometimes where the clouds seemed to part. As every sight or sound or thought or feeling seemed like a sign a pointer on this treasure map of your life. Everything seemed to have a hidden meaning. It was all examined, and judged. Am I doing it right or wrong? Is this helpful or harmful, good or bad? How am I? Where am I? When am I? Why am I?

And one morning as if by magic, the sun pierced your aching heart and the agony of knowing you were not one step closer to the elusive goal stole your breath. That's when the rains came, mountain storms held at arms reach for a lifetime, tsunamis of fear and despair and deep deep sadness crushed you and un-wove your fabric of dreams of a life of total sun. Of how you should be, of how life should be, of where you should be, or were...

You watched amazed as your foot falls dissolved as the path collapsed as the ground collapsed, and you realized there never was a mountain nor anyone to climb it. You discover to your utter delight and amazement and indescribable joy and overwhelming awe that all you had been looking for was already always the case. That the hinge pin to this smashing of the idea of inside and outside is the un-caused discovery that there are no things or non things. For what could not be perfect if there are no things, and what could not be peaceful if there are no edges nor split or division anywhere? What could not be at utter rest if there are no things to be moving nor non-moving?

All these ideas of other better and more or next are learned concepts to describe what cannot be described or caught with words or thoughts. All division was imagined, made up. You are also nothing more or less than a concept an idea that seemed to split apart this and that into the world and you. It always had been life doing itself, the seamless unknown vastness and simultaneously the worded world where there are mountains and paths and people to tread them. Trying Aching To reach the summit. The dream moves flows and there is not even nothing outside it. You are the dream, not the dreamer. This is it coyote.

Wordless wonder pools and swirls and slips softly into its own echo sliding through its unutterable undeniable aliveness it vibrates into song. Surging and cresting always the quivering tip of a wave falling between what has never been and what will never be. Made of memories and deep deep feelings and self referential thoughts shimmering without a center swirling cresting fading writing and erasing themselves. Arpeggio'd wonder in awe of itself. Life no longer owned, no longer longing for other as there is none. Simply an ache for the ache of whatever appears as it laughs and slides and sings and weeps and twirls in its own delight and amazement.

You are a tone poem a symphonic silence a passion play singing painting and erasing itself. Never touched never caught unbelievably marvelous and superb. Scrumptious tasty flavorful beyond measure

And what is the taste of taste, the touch of touch, this vibrant pulsating utterly obvious aliveness that has no name nor non name that you feel so intensely like magic under and beneath the imaginary lines and yet subsuming all and everything. No one knows but you are it and it is you. Naked unadorned unwavering pure stainless untouched awareness aware that it is aware through this dream play this magicians tale this fairy land of this and that and you and me

A call and answer sing song without a singer... of overtones of echoes pouring soaring in and through everywhere and no where. A shadow-less footless dance of all stepless steps bursting seemingly real yet made of imaginary seams ...coloring explosions imploding impossible unutterable songs of marvel where love and lover and the beloved kiss unceasingly without time or no time

As you are made up a dream an enchantment a spell cast upon the shimmering that skips your name across this rainbow iridescent dream scape rippling shine and shadow skimming flowing dissolving into the shores of this edgeless sea of dreams. An imaginary surface tension a temporary window between inside and outside between the physical world and the worded world between a characterless edgeless centerless a-temporal unknown unknowable and the known fabricated world of things. Between love and nothing at all

It's like you have a net and you're trying to catch the air but you cannot. No matter how high you jump or how far you reach, you cannot get outside of what's going on to capture it. But you know it's there it's here and you feel it deeply, this magic, and you want it. It's like you're trying to take all of the words and lines and letters of every treasure map you've read and stretch them into a long line, tie them altogether into a lasso and throw it up into the air so that it will capture moon light's song, the star shadow'd wonder. But it cannot, you cannot. You peered into the deepest darkest mirror and the clearest mountain streams with your heart in your mouth trying to find the source of the magic. And the ache for what you know not begins to eat you alive

And you begin to lose your footing and you reach out your hand to steady yourself and your hand falls through space through the light through the winds through the leaves and the lichens and the bark and the trees and the boulders and the ground as your feet dissolve in utter wonderment that there was never any mountain at all nor you to climb it or path to some sort of summit or goal or place to rest to land as inside falls through outside and up falls through down

All there is is an edgeless trembling shimmering scintillating light fabric not woven or composed or painted yet somehow sung of awe itself of echoed reflections of infinite timbre and hue of iridescent ephemeral unwritten shadows lit from within falling through itself of an indescribable limitless softness caressing itself embraced from the inside from the outside from sidelessness. A piercing brilliance coming from everywhere and nowhere has erased the imaginary shine and shadow of this and that and meaning and non meaning and place and placelessness ...yet there is dancing. And love

And you are the enchantment itself. Gazing out Gazing in... spellbound there are no words. Yet it sings itself. Without effort or non effort words slide through you pouring light through light no longer trying to grasp or ungrasp the magic you are it. It sings you

From the deepest darkest greeny blues of forest slumber to wind swept clouds of sunsets dream. No longer seeing through a veil of fear of falling as the falling is falling. No fear of unkowning as there is no one to know and no things to know. No fear of next, as time has died. No fear of death, as there is simply nothing left. Just an unowned uncaused centerless magnificence. Simply this obviously vibrantly alive self sprung self releasing naked unowned awareness knowing that it is aware through this transfixing dream that you are. Life shattered into a gazillion imaginary shards so it can see taste smell feel its own aliveness, see its own beauty, delight in its own delight, be amazed at its own amazement. Gaze and be spellbound by its own mystery and majesty.

This utter peace this ultimate stillness this all pervading awe is untouchable and uncaused. Unfettered by moonlight dreams of what's next or why or how. It's an un-contrived wow. And you are it

Butterfly reflections shimmer and sing and dance as sparkling. Their sh
them follow them swinging inbetween falling spiraling merging into and
own reflection. We swim in the shining imaginary echoed space between e   ...u
nothing, wall less mirrored canyons deeper than deep higher than high a breath a sigh
a hush a silence singing a symphony beyond composition we are fabricated dream nets
thrown over what cannot be found or touched or kissed or held or captured Life swoon-
ing into itself. Felt deeply. Piercing the ever emerging momentary with love's heart magic

like iridescent shadows tossing turning twisting twining streaming over and under into
and through each other disappearing and emerging at the same time impossible enchant-
ment born on wingless murmuring streams. Like echo'd reverberations not one without
the other never here without there a directionless placeless places colored in with flying
fleeting soaring whorls and swirls of worded worlds of woods and rivers and mountains
shining. A desert mirage vibrantly shimmering this wondrous dream seems to appear.

And thingness extends infinitely into Thinglessness. Exquisite fluted light feathered space
without end or beginning folding and unfolding into and through itself without sides or
edges beyond delicate scalloped soaring cloud dream'd castles growing and tumbling
blossoming and withering simultaneously

a touchless touch where everything and nothing fall through tumbled whirlpools of
bejeweled wonder... spied from a sideways glance an after thought an after image shim-
mers overtones of trails of empty footfalls of streaming colored echoes singing resound-
ing ricocheting reflecting a splendid fairytale an enchanted dream scape of things of you
of me of we. Sighing on the inbreath of nothing ...clear light reveals it's colors ...dancing
on the edge of a teacup ...the world appears as words paint themselves on the delicious
richness of unknowing

lost in the dream you look for a way out ...ladders to nowhere appear ...falling... made of
gossamer streams of thought they come apart as you touch them. all ideas of what this
is disappear as you lose yourself and lose the losing ripped into shreds love bleeds end-
lessly ...and colors appear in the brilliance of what cannot be touched or found or captured

and colorless drops of nothing break your heart forever ...no longer searching for mean-
ing or a source of unutterable priceless fleeting splendor ...words unowned skirt around
thingless beauty and fall magnificently short of ever kissing what can never be kissed
a flowing brushstroke of infinite color reaches through your heart and plays songs

reverberating with your being ...you watch the echoes falling softly through the canyon words flow through you and rivers and canyons appear ...sunlight streams upon your face. All evaporates as it blossoms ...leaving unfindable wakes of joy sliding back into the flowing the stars dance timelessly. With no idea of capture ...we are this un-named song as wind moves our hands ...love moves our hearts ...tears are the medium where we meet our reflections ...ahhhhhh even calling it wondrous ...falls short by infinite kisses

yet some are the songsters ...their steps are light ...they leave rainbows painted with emptiness hanging in the air

Knowing you are all made up knowing the dream is completely fabricated knowing that this is indeed it is marvelous beyond measure

First bedecked and then be-dazzled and then crushed crashed smashed to smithereens burnt up blown away. All ideas of this and that and truth and non-truth and meaning and non-meaning and choice and love dissolve. Until there is not even nothing left and you are suspended as nothingness. Either the fullness rushes in or it trickles back in, and you find yourself. Oh my! you're still here! Living and loving and laughing and sobbing. The full range of human emotion and experience. Life full on unadorned. Knowing you are the dream however makes all the difference. Knowing there is no escape. Knowing there is no one to escape. Suddenly all and everything is marvelous beyond measure as time has died there is no rush no urge for other for better for next.

Many of my words leave the mind hanging, with nothing to grasp. For how could the mind of this and that grasp what has no edges...

Tripling lightly adorned in sorrows embrace shadowed caverns hovered in a backwards glance neither fore nor hindsight offered a moments respite from a lifetime of wandering wondering where light sang sweetly like drifting moonlight o'er sands of memory not caught not lost nor island bound. glittering nets stranded in dawns mists forgotten by winds that had no need to arise or shine or fall through themselves lost in daylight found without hands or mind. Where did the poem you sought carry its beauty?

And tattered sails blushing in evening windsong, no hands at the helm no passenger within no direction to be found or lost in evenness endless blue up above fathomless blue below kissing in an embrace that flung oceans on the shores of seamless reflections where no harbor or place to rest lost a heartbeat. unfound in a bucket of midnight listing to no sides or shoulder where tears were not here nor there yet wetness everywhere and no where... the key was never hidden it simply never was in a pool of echoes starlight shimmered dancing through rippling moon song... a night hawk flew

and love wrote poems in the darkness as she mourned all that she had been ....the constant effort to find the essence of what she felt but could not capture. an indescribable magic had filled her emptied her left without hope or fear of life or death or love... unknown symphonies never written or heard yet always playing painting her love song with unutterable words... a pulse a heartbeat a vibration of overtones without a center never written never sung never woven nor undone, the skinless touch of this that never was and always is without time nor place filling everywhere and nowhere... echoed dream scapes rippling over shadows reflected in moonlight's glance... neither backwards nor sideways nor front and center... nor inside nor outside neither secret nor unhidden whirling twirling soaring streaming rushing roaring flowing feeling deeply yet not moving nor caught... a impenetrable darkness crushed all the light and blossomed into infinite petals of lovliness... the softness of unfindable taste and sound ...of seamless brilliance without gap or edge or feet to wander... silently singing brushing butterfly kisses as unwritten pages containing everything and nothing fly and disappear into vast spaciousness where they had never left

as what is going on is ambiguous sometimes words that leave the mind hanging... a love song... pierce us deeply for no reason for every reason and all stories lost in the hush of love's embrace words can take you to the edge... but what is there between the breath and the song... between a tear and it's wetness... where is the inbetween of inbetween? between you and me? and not even nothing is left to say yet we sing we are the song... as it sings itself... just. like. this

how could anyone feel so deeply love so much hurt so much without bursting? How could these feelings how could this precious humanness be owned? Where did she end and the sky begin? She reached out her arms to gather the stars and the night swallowed her and who woulda thunk that what we wanted so much was really nothing at all... so amazingly realer than real, intimate yet impersonal, an endless sigh falls through itself. A hush of sublime emptiness falling in love as origami hearts sail on a sea of dreams

and where was love's sideways glance? where was the heart he thought he had held in an empty glass? waiting for a kiss that would illuminate and pierce what could not be kissed, as starlight shimmered on the rim dancing on the infinite divide between here and no where... no need of words or song to sing of this love that holds you in its own embrace as empty handful of tears disappear into a bouquet of unutterable beauty. it is your gift to you it was a feather'd glance that stole his heart. He could not resist his shadow dancing... he found his will an empty letter cast with all his dreams into the sun where love lay bleeding, his heart adrift place-less arrows never shot yet pierced his dream of never forever collapsed into a wasteland, yet the sunset still beckoned filling empty sails with wakeless dreams of loves glimmering shadow

And in the hush of early early a wind sweeps across the night time dream and caresses her whispering kiss into a song where love appears like magic to bask in each other's glow. As shadow'd dreamscapes seemed to rise up to kiss an empty horizon where love lost his petaled glimpses of doorways beckoning into a time that time forgot. Whose feet wandered into deep tear'd forests submerged in desert sands? Whose song echoed forth in starlight wonder of days where nights stretched out their wings and embraced their tenderness as aching hearts spied their reflections and bled into the dream? Even love was a byline an empty space that collapsed into itself, as it blossomed into an empty shell and sung sea dreams where loves heart magic told its tale

every night fell through the day and left an impenetrable stillness that moved a stunning silence in waves of wonder, a brilliant thundering aliveness that spoke of nothing else than this indescribable vastness and a symphony without place or rhythm. yet unforgettably as fingerprints lost themselves in the whorls and swirls of the waves crashing at midnight on the shifting sands. Bathed in a kiss of moon.
Limitless cloud scapes never captured nor lost reflected in a sideways glance in flowing waters of supreme stillness echoed resounding ricocheting down wall-less canyons where shadows waltzed in timeless contrapuntal rhythms as infinite parentheses of primordial songs reverberate... stretching into an arabesque almost touching yet never touching nor not separate, consumed devoured in infinite spacious brilliance. Sky like vastness without other falls through itself collapsing ever blooming an implosion of exploding light swooning into light and color streaming through rainbow'd shimmering and sound falling through empty footfalls without border nor edge an unfindable unmissable point begins to draw lines through songs not sung never written yet inescapably wondrous......

morning sees itself bloom into day through a windowed glance where lips kissed ancient melodies into a song a breath a sigh falling back through itself. silent yet heard, slipping like wind through your fingers caressing your cheek your heart piercing like a saber shattering all your dreams of yesteryear and the morrow. time has lost and no one won slipping sliding dancing in as the flow ...bathed in sunsets dream... unknowing cannot be spoken of it is a sublime unknowing... without doubt or confusion or non confusion, words sing themselves and sing us into a painted flowing water color picture bleeding into a dream ...a river called time is needed for our tears to flood into and the rippling creates an ever emerging momentary that catches the sunlight ...just so and rocks and rolls and trickles and streams and dances and twirls into circles of whirlpooling shadows that eddy and flow into and through themselves. we are simply tone poems blossoming and falling aching for the light to strum our colors into streaming lanterns for just... a ...brief... moment... a window a touch a breath a sigh a moonbeam fell through her open door and wept on her doorstep... sobbing infinite colors and hues and uncountable inseparable oceans of light spilling flooding tasting touching aching for the taste of taste where life saw it self and was delighted and amazed at its own wonderment and sang and dove and slipped back into the flowing... back into the hush... back into the softness.... that you have always had been

melting... into your own caress... the inside dissolved into the outside this vibration this pulsating aliveness allowing awareness to be aware of itself and every note arching with innumerable overtones... creating a symphony, as silence and a hush and this breath that sing... music of unbearable beauty

you have become wonder itself... beauty looks in the mirror and weeps, slipping into and through each other... lost in the imaginary places in between... love is sublime, its like watching your lines form as the passion play sings and unsings itself being the character and watching it and knowing feeling that it is a dream and all your friends and lovers and that old man down the street are made up and love and madness continue... yet it is known they are also made up waltzing pirouetting dancing themselves into a world of separate things and ...time... a river a flowing where your tears can never be numbered or caught

and the sun could not see her infinite beauty but everywhere she gazed she saw her own reflection and the music sang itself ...waves formed and crashed onto the edges of a shoreless ocean.... and finding touching weeping into their own wetness dissolved into the sea
and when the lines are known and felt to be imaginary an unknowable beauty overwhelmingly naked and unadorned reveals itself... there is a direct intimate honesty as you no longer feel separate from what is going on... the made up world of things becomes unbelievably immeasurably wondrous the imaginary line between inside and out disappears

tears ... such unnameable beauty and what she could no longer name she felt surging through her as her it is uncontained unrehearsed uncaused ... you reach out your hands and the sky pulls you in.... you stretch your toes and the bottomless depths swallow you... and after you are consumed by the blueness you are forever part sky. it is the nakedness the rawness of life unowned... unhidden... not lost nor findable....... the dance where twoness slides into itself hearts touching falling dissolving... like this

Words jump out of the inky blackness and rainbows write symphonies across the sky that spill into your heart and dash against the sea leaving traceless rainbow reflections in your eyes arabesques in the sky left by the heron's wing ...not lost not found the sighs slip into the flowing... beauty reveals itself, never caught

like ripples flowing across fields of grasses never lost never found yet vividly apparent like the reflection of a kiss on an edgeless sea no lips can be touched. shadows dancing lost in a field of dreams found only in their rippling reflections and I have become the song I ached for and always seemed to miss, yet I could not quite recall the words, they were always on my lips, the taste of taste the warm liquidity the ever present flowing of home. This vibrant pulsating aliveness that you feel moving through you. Is you. Isn't it amazing that we, as a product of the thought stream, can watch it paint a symphony of colors arpeggio and fall

blooming in infinite incomparable forms merging flowing rippling shimmering into and through castles of ever moving clouds and thought dreams and pictures and sounds of pasts and futures and stories of brilliant immediacy shooting through edgless space and stopping pausing... hanging by threads of weaving bejeweled wonder illuminating the inky darkness seeming to settle, and Rocket again into dancing shadows lit from within shot through with myriad unfindable specks and sparkles of hints of weightiness of the enormity of utter lightness and oh my! Deep feelings that run and sparkle and pierce the day, and a you that is not separate from the forces blooming and falling, and that this pulsating aliveness you feel you know so intimately so tenderly so wondrously shooting through you, is you

And empty winds blew through the morning and echoed songs into the vastness of love and love lost and shadows dancing in the night. Neither here nor there nor lost nor found. Waves crash on the edge of a shoreless ocean and without any hope of harbor her heart sank. The stillness of evening rose in the ripple less wake of dawn. Colors shapes timbre and hue drop from unfathomable depths and sing into form and fade simultaneously

The scaffolding the myriad planes of an ever shifting dance floor fall away and there is no more place to hang your hat .....no corner no center no edge can be found. starlight weeps at its own magnificence as it sweeps through your skinless mind. Falling through the mirror everything and nothing must go. But a reflection of who you were, a shadow, a phantom dances. Lit by shimmering starlight a pas de deux sings us into being

Simultaneously disappearing merging dissolving emerging breaking the surface of the ocean like a manta ray shimmering in the sunset. Rainbows streaming down and through transparent mind. Joyfully playing in the waterland of love. Delightfully sliding down the curl of duality the thought stream is constantly creating you ...but there is a knowing that it is a creation and that it is ever fleeting and has no substance. Just as the wind makes no imprint on the sky. Yet you fly as the wind as the wind blows through you at the same time. Riding the up-drafts of love. Swirling dancing in ever widening spirals of ecstasy

and sometimes when you're surfing you can reach out and touch the side of the wave... fingers dipped in swirl, and sometimes when you least expect it the sun shines right through you, and sometimes when the package you tried to stuff your afflictions in comes undone... the wave swallows you and sometimes... as if by magic... the magic unties you and sometimes... your reaching fingers...stretch into an arabesque quite marvelous... is no longer separate from the moon and the hush of midnight is your very breath and the roar of canyon winds ... sings your name... as it sails through your hair your skin your teeth your blood your bones... and you are the wind and the wind is you and you realize it has always been this way

your very heart your very love explodes into the night... and your heartbeat is every-where... this and that... magnificently unfolding... weaving and unweaving the dream the dance the song... with jewels of tears like rain like sorrow like joy like nothing at all. an empty breath subsides into the sand glistening in the sunset on the edge of a shoreless ocean ... where even love cannot find a harbor... all anchors have been ruptured like the sails of her dreams... tattered flying magnificently in uncharted seas. This vibrant pulsat-ing aliveness that you feel moving through you Is you

And he longed to bathe in starlight, but his skin was in the way. He could not rip it off as it was him And he longed to sing like starlight, but his mouth was in the way. He could not remove it as he was the words. Suddenly without warning starlight swallowed him. Neither here nor there Neither lost nor found. Homeless mind feelings happen... yet there are no feelings until named... no separate feelings until named... no separate you having feelings until named... there are simply so separate things... until named... no you ...no me... no love... life happens utterly spontaneously yet it has no name nor non name

all separation is made up... conceptual... what is going on has no qualities or characteristics or measurement or split or division or edge anywhere... and as soon as one word is spoken or thought... it is like a lightening bolt has ruptured the vault of unending sky into infinite shards of blue... and every piece feels like a dagger in your heart... because as soon as the concept the idea of you arises, you now feel separate from what is going on and you spend the rest of your life trying to feel whole to patch what was never separate... and everything you do ...all seeking searching for that missing peace... merely perpetuates the illusion of separation... tightens the noose... as belief in separation is the same as belief in personal volition... you will not find the answer to this problem in a book... or in a poem... or meditation... or falling in love... or walking in nature... although these may seem to give you a temporary sense of relief... the permanent relief you seek will cost you everything and nothing... yet you cannot choose to pay

it is a ripping apart of everything you have held to be true about yourself and the world... including the idea of truth... and love... and purpose and meaning... it is a most perilous journey... that no one can choose... as there is no path to no where... and no one can give you nothing... and no one arrives.... you will never get this... it is truly an empty prize for no one

and when unicity becomes obvious you are not thinking, "oh I am inseparable from the tree or the sky or my neighbor" ... there simply is no you and tree and space inbetween,,, no before or after like pegs on a line of time. It is not "Oh! I am all this!" or even "All this!"

it is known and felt that there are no separate things or events, time and self and other never existed. there is not even nothing until thought seems to create it. This is always known to be a dream. Yet somehow realer than real as wordless wonder is always on, brilliant and beautiful underneath the storm it cannot be thought about or spoken of... the tightly clenched fist of I am explodes into everywhere and no where... its not that the hand unfolds, it becomes transparent

Believing in the dream Is the dream. Knowing it is a dream Is the dream. Recognizing and feeling unicity Is the dream. Believing you can escape Is the dream. Knowing you cannot

Is the dream. Believing in other in time in separation Is the dream. Knowing this is it Is the dream ... All require imaginary separation. Anything said about the dream is the dream. All description Is the dream. Including this.

What is going on is spontaneously naturally present. Without any doing or non-doing it is obviously so. A vast expanse it cannot be contained or captured as it has no edges or center or any place or thing that can be grasped. Limitless it cannot be imagined or thought about or conceived of in any way. It is pure and unstainable and cannot be added to or subtracted from. We all know this as it is deeply intuited. Yet the apparent arising of self and all other things seems to hide this unutterable knowing ness. this recognition of unicity cannot be contrived or arrived at as it is already the case. As long as there is belief in separation there will be an attempt to reconnect that which has never been separate.

One tries to imagine this feeling of oneness and creates a goal that seemingly can be attained. Yet that idea of oneness is simply that, an idea. As all ideas of future attainment merely perpetuate the feeling of going somewhere, and the illusion that there is a you that can do something to get there. But there is no future, it is an idea. Past is merely memories occurring in the Ungraspable unfindable inseparable momentary. There nothing outside of this nor things inside, yet it contains and includes all thingness. It simply cannot be grasped or understood as there is no separate grasper or things to be grasped. It is not an it nor a non it. There is no outside to what is going on and no inside, there is no other, not one not two not none.

This is it always. Just as it is. Looking for it is included, as well as the recognition of it. Life simultaneously writing and erasing itself. Of itself so. Knowing this intellectually will not stop the seeking for it. Seeking is a perpetually self sustaining loop. Something else uncaused happens that breaks the circling the spinning in which an imaginary center arises.

If even if the words we use to describe this vast uncompounded limitless expanse are beyond imagining than how could what's going on be within the realm of imagination? As it is like a dream, like an illusion, like a hologram like a mirage, like an echo a reflection. No word concept idea can touch it grasp it kiss it. Yet it includes all words and descriptions. Edgeless seamless infinite centerless indivisible with no reference points whatsoever. Yet vividly apparent all things seem to arise that have no independent existence. Like imaginary castles in the air you cannot move in, like a mirage in the desert you cannot drink from it, like a reflection of your lovers face in the mirror you cannot kiss it, as space cannot be grasped, and you can never find harbor on a shoreless ocean. There is nothing to be gained by looking for fulfillment in an empty glass that has no bottom or sides or emptiness and you cannot fill something which has no space to be filled.

Even as things seem to arise they are merely made up as what is going on cannot be divided. There are no things no non things that can change or not change, move or not move. There is no one to be free or not free. Here nor there as there is no place nor non place. No time nor timeless ness. No inside nor outside, nor both nor neither. There are no separate things to be lost, and no one to find them.

There is no one to put together what was never separate. All dream trying perpetuates the illusion of a trier and a goal of wholeness. As wholeness cannot be imagined as it has no edges. It remains an idea a goal to reach in the nonexistent future. The trying is like the prow of a ship pretending to slice up the sea.

The painful feeling of separation creates the urge to somehow find oneness, yet oneness is an idea.
The closest the intellect can get is inter-relatedness. It is not possible to believe or understand or imagine that there are no things.its like the words slide off the mirror and you fall through...
every shard piercing your heart, and you realize that the sky was never broken, and your heart was never yours...

It's like a rawness isn't it, this deep deep feeling, so intense, so so so beautiful. It's our very humanness, and excruciating when you're trying to name it or figure it out or get rid of it or change it. As soon as you try to change it or figure it out, there appears a struggler a namer. The pain of imaginary separation appears when the labels are seen and believed.

No one can choose to stop trying!
As long as you feel separate you will try to patch yourself or the world together or look for a meaning or some reason or rhyme. A glue called understanding that you can use to put all the pieces together so you can feel whole.
Yet have you ever been separate from these feelings? Is there a you having them? Can you choose them?

Or is it life uncaused, simply flowing as it does? This un-namable dancing we call life includes everything doesn't it? It can look and feel like anything, utterly beautifully unpredictable and precious beyond measure.

What we call emotion is such an extraordinary expression, an infinitely petaled flower that blooms simply for no reason or non reason. I see the utter beauty, the magnificent transience, the unknowable ness, beyond comprehension, and there is no urge to try to measure the vastness. it has no edges or corners, there is no place to hide. This is it, And it is you.

Here are your feet walking on the ground with these universal wings outstretched, soaring to nowhere from everywhere.
you have never left home and you have never been bound nor free...
you are the wind and the wind flows through you, you are life as life flows through you as you, beautifully magnificently so.

and lilting melodies of forgotten futures fall softly into your heart.
exempt of hopes and fears you swirl into the vastness and you cannot find your head.
Folded into your colossal all encompassing heart is all that there is, forever undone, forever collapsing into itself is your amazing love light shining brilliantly beautifully as you.

You may call it love and you may call it emptiness and you may call it wonder and you may call it sorrow or joy, and you may call it anything at all and yet this ache, this most beautiful beautiful ache we all know it don't we?

It is the fiber of our emptiness it is the fiber of our fullness and it is the fiber of our being.
Nakedly adorned in silent wonder
life sings, and we appear.

How amazing to discover that life happens as it does, not as it is supposed to do, but just as it seems to. No one or thing makes it happen.
I never believed in God, and yet I did believe in personal volition. There was a lot of pain believing that there was a me who had a choice, that there was someone actually doing life. Yet all the time deep down recognizing that if indeed there were a controller life certainly would not feel this way. I certainly would have chosen fluffy nice thoughts and emotions!

Untangling dreams of empty shadows, Leaves fall.
Without intent. Tears fall.
They have no name, or target.
Yet we know their beauty.

brilliant unadorned naked emptiness

flowing naturally. vast unclouded unfettered sky. seamless ease abides. without any effort, without any non effort, life flows.

Feeling this knowing this deeply that life does itself the mind is embraced with a clear spacious luminosity.

There is no longer trying to find a place to rest or question what has no answer.

silence sings.

and the sea birds seemed to hover as they swam through the evening skies, and without a whisper they swooped and swirled and headed into the night.

and you feel your heart maddened by the beauty of the fleeting winds

and there is no more rage to change it or cast your dreams into the sea.

For your footfalls are enchanted with a shadow's cry of the delight of darkness.

and as she sang brushstrokes of emptiness dipped in shadow'd reflections sighed a hue of rainbow tears. She spoke in tongues where no one could peer into the words.

As watercolored dreamscapes rippled over and under and through each other there was a hush, a deeply penetrating loveliness where time died and an unspeakable magnificence was undeniably singing.

As echoes ricochet in reverberating parentheses lassoed dreams like footfalls from the past dissolved in timeless wonder, she spied a shadow fanning along a path she had forgotten.

tears still flowing mightily rushing and roaring streaming soaring flying in wakeless thunder longing to kiss the silent sea.

as she had slipped into the liquidity of her flowing reflection she lost herself on the other side, and mountains peered behind the cloudburst waltzing cascades of empty rhymes. They formed her as she dissolved into them. The song needed no language yet it was deeply felt. Unsung it sang itself...

And Sounded Like This.

and this urge that is me to sing of what cannot be sung, to kiss what cannot be kissed, to dance a dance that would whirl my lovers into awe of their own magnificence floods these pages with words that have no meaning.

an iridescence a shimmering a ripple in the darkness, a heartsong that cannot be captured and tried on like a feathery dress, that might cause you to soar.
yet I sing and I dance and I twirl and I weep, knowing it is only love in verse in meaningless rhythms with no rhyme.

a sweet melancholia sweeps through you and stirs up forgotten motes sparkling in your heart ....shimmering and dancing your old songs on an empty stage... It strikes deeply in the most intimate part of you ...it is neither bad nor good ....an indefinable falling through yourself ....as you are ripped inside out you lose direction and no longer care which way is up, Or down. Life soars through you as you.

He followed his tears to the ocean, vast... he scanned and could see no things and all there was was a sunset blooming, reds and oranges danced in the sky that had swallowed him. He tried to rip the bandages from his tattered heart looking for true love, and every ounce of effort built the remnants of his castle higher and higher. What would he be without the trying? Where would he be without a castle and clouds and a song to follow? Without a belief in home? He twirled and he stumbled and he fell upon himself. there must be, there had to be someplace where he could rest! yet everything he touched began to crumble every star every lover every tear every moment. His own reaching began to fall apart, his own fingers begin to lose their focus... he could not remember what he was reaching for or why, and his reasons fell into the vastness. what was the time what was the place where was the morrow? where was that last place that he thought he had glimpsed a certain brightness a certain luminosity that pierced his heart? was it not now was it not always was it not always... was it past was it not future..... where was the clock where was his timeline where were his fingers where was his heart... where was his song where was the love... where was the where when even nothing was lost

And what would it be if there was only the cricket song... if tears washed away your footprints... if light burned away your shadow... where does a dance go when it has no steps... why is a song when it is silent

and what can I say what do I long to say what do I long to share how how can I share this, kiss this, it is your kiss, these lips are your lips, this love is your love and it has always been this way and it will always be. although there is no time, you are not lost you are not found, you do not exist, you are but a memory of an aching heart, you are but a dream of a song of a memory that sang so sweetly. A reflection in the night where shadows died, lilting refrains echoing down the canyon washing moonbeams of emptiness into a basin that has no bottom... we are but tears falling from an empty sky and knowing this there is nothing more sublime.

and he crawled across the burning desert tried to drink from every mirage until every pore of his being was ripped inside out and he stood amazed at his utter nakedness and wept as the full moon sailed through him

Overwhelming unbearable beauty shimmering shining baseless directionless reflections echoing from nowhere from everywhere, Exploding imploding a timpani a solo a duet a chorus of one of two of many of none ....a cacophony of wonder a symphony a song who's words can never be heard but our felt deeply always whose melody sings you sings me sings silence breathing. a stillness of utter magnificence moving without movement, overtones and undertones with infinite reverberations a kaleidoscopic Wonderland. An ever blooming flower extending everywhere and nowhere simultaneously .....in all direction in no direction touching itself in these rhythmless rhythms these patternless patterns ...an exquisite dance singing itself. Wind and light and life flowing through me as me. Kissed embraced from the inside from the outside there are no sides there are no non-sides it is softer than soft, This edgeless life, This transparent seamless beingness

This ease of life doing itself. No more backwards glances to see where footsteps lie. They all filled with tears long ago and the edges crumbled. No more wondering where these foot falls will go. There is no direction there is no next longed for. The dance knows how to dance when the dance floor has fallen away and you looked at your dance card and you realize it has always been empty. It is always the first and last kiss

my own sweet love, My own I's sparkling with tender wetness allowing the primordial preverbal unknowable unsingable un-catchable all encompassing hum ....the vibration the heartbeat of existence allows life to sing to taste to Touch to feel its own aliveness... vibrantly passionately beautifully in love with love, in awe of awe. How marvelous that these words can flow through me and paint my imaginary lines just as they self erase, For when I am not singing of this there is simply suspended edgeless awe.

And randomly spiraling drifts of daydream gossamer spiderwebs soaring through the air, Catching the light in sparkling radiance. Threads forgotten untied the light, Burning brightly through ideas of time aloft adrift suspended as nothingness. Dawn sees itself in the morning flower. Wind kisses itself in the petals. shimmering Tears touching the radiance between light and shadow seeing their Reflection in the canyon stream. Echoed halls of wordless wonder. Wandering meandering ricocheting Soundlessly singing. The day begins Lost in night Lost in light... Swooning into and through itself, Caressed from the inside out the universe swallows me falling into my own infinite intimate embrace

its like the sea collapsed into the sky and crushed you and you drowned, and you awaken rolled up onto an empty beach... surf playing in your toes and seaweed in your hair... and there is no difference between you and the sea or sky or sand or before or after.... and slowly softly you can see shells sweeping in and out, and you can discern clouds forming echoing the shallow sea foam dancing... and your hand enjoys the warm wet sand that your tears have joined into a concert of wonder... and this peace of belonging of home of utter rest never leaves... and you walk down the empty beach naked unadorned in utter wonder one foot ever sliding into the vastness the other footless in the sand

that all consuming final tsunami of night crashes into you crushes you on the rocks and corals and drags you out into the bottomless depths until all that you were is squeezed out of you. As a centerless light appears erasing the shadows of apparent duality. Flooding you consuming you in an enormity of sublime lightness. Transparent seamless beingness never leaves even after you are spit out again. Aching. On the shore Of wet and dry Up and down, Here And There

Thoughts words concept ideas can never capture what is going on as what is going on is fluid and has no edges, yet they paint a beautiful picture of separate things and separate colors and separate people and separate moments and separate feelings. Weaving a beautiful web that seems to catch for an instant time place dimension causality love and beauty. But this web of words this dream of separation is magnificent when it is not believed in, however when it is believed in it it is exceedingly painful.

Scarab shattered on the rails of infinity... Greenie golds orange-ing into purply skies the sublime hush of nighttime swoons into the arms of day... collapsing under its own weight lightness breathes a sorrowed gasp of wonder twisted and turned wrenched and plummeted into itself aghast unstrung untangled in the tangles and deep marrowed webs of its own magnificence

And what was it. What was the Lure, what was the song what was the carrot the golden ring that was dangled just beyond your grasp? You knew that it was huge beyond infinite, and you knew that it was a mystery that could never be grasped. You knew that it was a majesty that laid you bare. Stripped of everything, Stripped of nothing, the longing to collapse into your own magnificence. Pounded you Be-jangled you. Ripped you. Tore you shredded you. Pierced you at the very center until the center exploded. Your head underwater on the shore, the waves beat you flattened you. Between movement and non movement there was no longer a space, or place to find comfort to find safe harbor. To find purchase on the rocks of this shoreless sea their resonance overwhelmed any ideas of rhythm or ryhme.

It was the music the hush of the universe laughing weeping sobbing at its own beauty. you finally caught a glimpse of yourself reflected in your own tears in the waves in the ocean in all wetness, In all tenderness, In every human as every story unfolding infolding. Rapt at the unwrapping of amazement. Tangled untangling this map of silence begins to sing anew always this touch this taste this sound... this life this life this life this life untold... sings itself

Filigreed light wings caress'd the window where his heart waited for his lover ...but she crept in the back door a shadow an echo a memory... as he turned and colors swirled and danced in a mirage of an embrace like autumn leaves suspended in a hush. he reached to touch to grasp to to merge with the song he knew so well but had seemed to have forgotten ...and the rhythm moved him deeply... pierced that waiting heart indefinable words of a familiar sound wove into enchanted beauty. Transfixed, he no longer cared to find the melody the song the dance the beauty the magnificence. He understood it was not separate from him. As the wind left a trace in the room where love died. Reflections blossoming in an empty bouquet

She spun in every direction trying to hear to catch the primordial song without words, and was overwhelmed when her heart was pierced from the inside from the outside, Echoes gleaming in the wasteland of love. A cat's cradle crocheted of dreams and fears and yesteryears tears could not capture the light as it fell through the apparent shadows of diversity, revealing an ancient wonder that could not be kissed. In the end there is simply an a temporal kiss, a contrapuntal timeless blast of silence singing, a continual union of what was never separate. And the ever emerging self releasing momentary is unbearably wondrous. All we can know but not grasp is this magical symphony playing itself as it self releases.

All your hopes and dreams and expectations of what life looks like what it should look like vanish. life is a trackless wonderland. Smoke signals in the dark, The scent of wonder blossoms

All we can know, all we can feel, is this utterly obvious always on unavoidable brilliant aliveness. This edgeless beginning-less endless a temporal uncatchable unpinpointable fleeting without ever existing, simultaneously emerging and self erasing like a measure-less limitless infinitely varied explosion imploding without variation..... this ambiguous amorphous ever emerging momentary... a surge a bursting an infinitely blooming flower weeping dissolving tenuously beautifully impermanent ...nor impermanent. Writing itself on a river lost in whir-pooled reflections like shadows flowing over and under into and through each other on rippled sourceless shimmering

It is a beautiful sublime melancholy as you have lost everything including someone who can lose or gain anything or nothing. Even love

And awakening is really nothing at all, But it far exceeds any ideas of what you thought you wanted. There can be endless tears as Joy and sorrow merge into a supreme deep current of unnamed unowned emotion. There is a simple joy in just being feeling. No one to care what it might be labeled.

And driving in the late afternoon sun the pavement is so beautiful It takes your breath away. All of it so wondrous Utterly beyond belief or understanding... the shhhhhhhhhh of, Oh my! How could it be so unbearably marvelous. And there is no one left to ask, Or answer

In the deepest dark of the night there is an undeniable stillness a hush... winter approaches the cricketsong left with the last moon like a dream or a vision... you can't quite forget or remember the story or song but the melody penetrates your being. a vibration a hum a calling you beckoning you from the inside from the deepest hidden unseen part of you that you try to deny it demands attention. Yet when you try to see it to capture it It van-ishes... Like an echo reverberating pulsating vibrating all and everything moving as this dance extending farther than you can see or imagine or imagine you can imagine.

the ocean birds shadow soars across the brilliant rippling waters and you look up to find. Nothing. a cloud seems like a landmark in a storm but your feet find no purchase on the reflections from yesteryear, and you can no longer find your shadow as your story has unfolded into the vastness of all stories, a single tear wet like wetness a drop of rain slides into the sea never not wet. This Glistening tender wetness of our beautiful shared humanness.

Unwritten stories write themselves. Dancing footless as starlight's echo bathed in the warmth of the moon's reflection, Spinning in the spin of what she no longer cared to catch. Her rainbow skirts fell into the sky. Trailing into infinitely cascading filigreed wonder kissing all and everything into a stream of delight. There is a timeless ease, the back beat of this unwritten symphony whispering baseless overtones, a wordless wonder sings.

not related nor intertwined.... an edgeless emptiness subsumes and unties all ideas of need for completion, she was a hologram of an endless bow on a package sent to no one twisting and curling exploding chrysanthemum ribbons of sky, and the empty box bereft of wishes and dreams was the prize. the present unwrapped itself and revealed gifts beyond imagination. The shock of recognition, The Zing of what can not be captured, the brilliance of seamless transparency caught in a glance From the side of a rearview mirror, simply so it reveals itself, spontaneously singing itself, as it immediately falls into its own hush... Just Like This

the paint had fallen off the glass and the light and love she had longed for pierced shattered her and scattered her tears like infinitely faceted gems throughout all and everything, and everywhere she looked she saw her own starlight dancing. And everything she touched she felt her own warm tears. she was the scent of scent the blue of blue the touch of touch. More intimate than her tongue in her mouth... an unbearable joy knowing that she was unknowable flooded through her night and day... and she wept

writing backwards a cross the sky torn up in dreams reflection ripping away everything and nothing, Jewels gleaming untouched uncapturable facets cut through their own reflections, like a knife in the soft palate of your heart tasting the fullness you dream of more, and you are lost forever in your desire to know to capture to hold the unholdable, until the spark the ember the fire burns your hand, Burns to the ground and your ashes are swept away, and only a memory can rebuild reform nothingness into you now ... spaceless beingness

like a reflection on a ripple an echo in a dream there's nothing to find and no one to find it... this lostness beyond lost or found is sublimely okay. There is no concern to capture the light. It is obvious that it's everywhere like a centerless jewel you are the reflections dancing streaming light streaming space streaming stories across the universe a shooting star in all its glory has no comparison to you

a stillness that sings without a singer it appears without any effort or non effort, and is recognized without and effort or non effort. All arising equally and evenly and self releasing without ever existing a song that moves and swings without movement dancing...

An uninterrupted indivisible seamless symphony a flow of what we call perception, Feeling sight sound taste bodily sensation touch, and the simultaneous inseparable recognition of it. We are that flowing without movement, That song without melody, We emerge in the thought stream that sings us into being. This passion play painting and erasing itself ...pure vast spacious beyond measure. We are the light and the reflection. The hush falls through the hush in between the breath and the song. we are that love song. Life kissing itself through our lips, Singing itself, Weeping at its own measureless supreme beauty, Shimmering awe. Like this.

And she ran with utter abandon no longer caring of the hurt or love she felt she had lost, and she felt that thick coat slip off her shoulders, and wings grew out of the ashes of that tightness that constriction. No longer running to or from the lightness of her footsteps... her breath the wind. The memory of tears paled, Time was lost, Wondrous beingness known utterly. Stunned that the searchlights of hope and fear no longer pinned her to the ground. Like a wild child born to no one fresh roots exposed to the light. This nakedness is astounding. Everything we thought we didn't want a world of what we considered to be affliction like a can opener rips yer socks off every last corner turned inside out

Walking in wonder... The streetlights are your clothes they swirl around like empty dresses and brush your tender cheeks with nothing other than your own heartfelt kiss. This current of love seems dreamlike as it is like nothing you've felt before. life can no longer be put into boxes where you kiss the lock and throw away the key.

Nothing is saved or earned in this flowing edgeless dream. oil lamps are no longer lit ... waiting for your lover to come home. No longer do you wait for that dragon's breath on your cheek, yet your lips smile at the memory, And you cry remembering the pain of waiting...... For an impossible dream for a four leaf clover to grow in your heart and alight the way to freedom to love to peace. Counting the stars till midnight and never knowing where to start to break open the sky so love will never be missed. No longer waiting for a lonesome ship to sail into your heart no longer hoping to be wed with the captain, there is no one manning the boat as seas softly stirring form whirlpools of emptiness

Its like every dream unfurled yet like nothing at all when your heart drops there is only a sublime ripple in the air... Like a breath... Not yours or mine, an ever heard never sung song singing the moment into existence ...the wind blows through you, and you are the wind dancing. Tears flow through you and the world is weeping. They slip into the imaginary spaces between us where love ignites, Washed in ringlets of dew set adrift gossiping among the stars

It's a shimmering dancing with no shadow casters yet the light seems to swirl in and around and through you, the puppet master lost his bet and ran screaming into the darkness he cannot be found he was a mirage, Just like you

and no longer looking for that which cannot be found even a touch a moment a kiss a glance A sigh the evening calls you Into the dance, Brilliant baseless beingness there is really no ultimate cause no separate events or things it's all of a piece..... And yes it's all description, stories, how beautiful that the mind can make up these stories of lovers of fighters and a sun that lies below the horizon waiting to rise ...Wakeless streaming rainbows falling into themselves laughing

One never needed to see where the sky kissed the sea, it was your own moon rising in the unfathomable sea of tears where you drowned, So beautiful this delicate transience, a rippling of the wind opens the curtains just for a moment... Loose strands of my hair caress my cheek, Songs write themselves. Laughing winds crying, Swimming in pools of moonlight where safety and danger have merged

Teardrops waving... Collapsing into themselves, bottomless Spilling flowing toppling the firmest foundation this water of love ripping the heart of the universe out and spreading it across the heavens... and dying the fabric of earth with indelible kisses that fade into the moon. Songs unheard songs never written kiss you full on the mouth. The kiss of nothingness erases time yet it is written with forgotten melodies as it re appears smiling... in every touch every gesture... every breath sings this is it it has always been this way

And he looked for what was under his shadow, behind the word, there was no non-word. memories of night time dreams waltzed with daytime dreams like morning mist dissolved in the light of day, swirling like a ghost a phantom kiss of darkness. As dreams of finding the essence of life, A truth or meaning he could hold. a gem a jewel a magical incantation began to wander down ancient paths and fell into the abyss where he had glimpsed his reflection. It was a ghostly breath that had haunted him his entire life that longing for certitude..

And without longing for a place to land there was no one to land. The Constant urge to find the treasure dissolved when he found that he was the treasure. there was no more longing for a magical kiss That which he had felt was on the tip of his tongue swallowed him. Unspeakable unbearable beauty flooded the dream and a hush a sigh a stillness penetratingly magnificent sang saturated with lightness and wonder. There is no path across the great desert dream. All imagined walking leads in circles following sign-less signs into grooves that get deeper and deeper and perpetuate the illusion of a center, An inside and outside...

Some whilst walking find their clothes falling off... their skin and lips and teeth and bones and hearts torn asunder..... smiles and tears filling their footsteps..... And as they reach the edge of the known world they see.... a great unknowable infinite vast spaciousness.... ravishingly beautiful... For most it is too terrifying and they run ... gathering their clothes

For a very few the sun and wind and supreme vastness is undeniably unbearably beautiful, and they live beautifully balanced on the edge, Dancing on the edge of a feather between the dream of love ...and the delicious magnificence of knowing that there are no things to know, no one to know anything, and nothing,,, not even nothing at all

It was a trick of the light, a shadowy dance that seemed to illuminate a piece of the path where she walked every morning to gather water from the river. It captured her, held her, this magic spell, this enchantment. She knew that if she could just remember the dance the steps from her dream, she would know, touch, kiss, the essence of love...

Turning and twisting and flowers in her hair, favorite pebbles smoothed from her pockets, songs that seemed to drift from no where, presents given to no one, waiting for no thing, but this.

The wave rises, shimmering light gathers through transparent greens, and her heart rode on the crest. Ever emerging, always falling, the awe the thrill... the rush! of this constant union of what was never apart. This and that seem to appear, tree tops dancing in the wind, we are the shoreless ocean and the edges between. Folding into your colossal all encompassing heart is all that there is, yet forever undone.

Like a song you sang long ago,
it whispers your name in the wind dancing across your ears. It is right around every corner, just missed. Your tongue seems to miss the taste, your heart aches to hear it again. You know this treasure has to be right here because you have looked everywhere for it. One day perhaps you hear the song you have always sung.

The hum of shadows Spinning through eternity. Colors dancing through infinite facets of this center-less jewel That you are.

Echoes flew down the canyons of ricocheted reflections as the hum of overtones penetrated the silence that sang of a heartbeat in the forest.

An imaginary weaving of light streaming and dancing as winds reflection super saturated kaleidoscopic colors swirling seemingly catching light in overflowing cups of wonderment.
Amorphous ambiguity swimmingly soars as there are no reference points whatsoever. The very impermanence the fleetingness that we feared becomes the treasure.

We are the words. Hollowed out echoes resounding in bamboo chords.

Cascading tears down echoed canyons without hope of relief without fear of stillness. Knowing the searing desert will dry up all this wetness... The beauty of the dancing mirage that you believe will give you water, respite, Solace, and an end to your thirst and tears.

This virtual reality filled with Thick and thin threads crocheting empty dreams as they unwind themselves as they nearly form. A tight woven sweater hung from the clothesline. Wind and sun beat up on it until all the wetness was gone. Oh my! What would you be without your tears? How could you hug without sleeves? ...tears, the very essence of wetness, cannot be captured as they flow into the ocean of dreams.

Primordial dreamscapes paint a picture of rainbow'd teardrops glistening in the deepest night. Swirling in eddies and whirlpools meandering. There is no one crossing the desert dream. And yet we die.

And moonlight streamed through her. A Shadows glance sang of Rip tides and whirlpools and shimmering eddies that reflected an unknowable self illuminating wonder in darkened edgeless seas. Waves crested mightily. A silent thunder roared.

shattered rainbow shards glimmered showering rhythm into the empty vastness without beginning or end, and a dream a dance of you and me invited my heart to sing.

We are that pure unstainable endless perfect brilliance and simultaneously indivisibly the infinite blooming flower of all and everything. Shimmering iridescent reflections swirling around an empty center as all imaginary thingness seems to arise, vibrantly apparent yet having no independent existence. Without time not non time nor place nor non place. We are an illusory reference point around which all conceptual things swirl, creating a virtual reality, A magicians tale, Life itself can see Touch Hear Feel It's own aliveness through the magic of your beautiful humanness. We are but a brief window of life seeing itself.

There is no ultimate understanding. It is more of a delicious unknowing ...seeing the world with baby eyes..... And all need vanishes.... including the need to know. your eyes licked clean of a lifetime of hope and fear. It is unstoppable it is ungraspable..... It's not an it nor a non it. Try to grab a moment and put it somewhere, find the beginning and end to a moment. There is no separate moment and no location... there is nothing other than this looking and feeling like anything at all ...including thinking it's something else. abounding awe and profound uncaused peace pervade

and waves of desert sand blow into swirls of sunburnt clouds obscuring the sun.... and the universe wrings itself out and torrents of sorrow and despair wash the sand into rivulets that flow into the ocean of joy.... and crystal clear brilliance tumbles into itself.... radiating pure love magic bursting into endless multi-petaled flowers.....

I cannot find a past or future yet I am made of memories... Fleeting spiraling tastiness of life touching feeling itself through the lens of our beautiful humanness

Drops reflecting your beauty streaming down your face and body. Folding into and through themselves flowing into footsteps where love lost itself on a path that had no wanderer or goal. Sweetness of salty tears sublimely merging in the vast depths of endless ocean song. Like a breath of sunlight streaming through you, Piercing your heart and every secret corner of your being with a fullness that explodes into everywhere and nowhere. Not lost nor found the fullness of perfection has no lack. This sublime resounding emptiness overflows...

And you are the wind and the sand and the sky and the waves and the caress and the hush before Dawn. And you are simultaneously everything And nothing at all, Waves flowing caressing their own wetness reflecting light from within without, the hush the silence the song of perfect un-namable undeniable brilliant vast spacious stillness is always on Singing itself, Just, Like, This

Melodies paint colored echoes in silent sky rippling in song bursting into bloom... flowing falling weeping wilting weaving un-weaving light dreams in the night... gleaming overtones crocheted her heart unleashed into the flowing fabric where she last saw it as it dipped into moonlights dance, dropping her dance-card, losing her step, losing her feet as the dance floor collapsed in wonderment

No longer trying to count the stars she was swallowed by sky. As waves crashed into limitless heavens swooning through an ease a hush that fell though itself, love lay bleeding and could not be rescued or gathered or held as it was no longer hers. Life, an infinitely faceted centerless jewel spinning itself weaving and unweaving. folding and unfolding simultaneously, breathing itself in waves of wonder arising and dissolving. Blooming and withering with no place to land, nothing solid or stable or fixed an ease of flowing daydream revealing itself without any effort, without anything needing to be done.

longing to fall and longing to be held, it is this longing that rips you to shreds and pierces you deeply shattering every dream of love. pulling every secret corner of your being inside out. your heart drops and you become the song you longed for, as it paints itself into echoed shadows silently dancing singing loves dreams into an illuminated flowing embrace you have fallen into and through. you are the inside and out of your own caress. you are your perfect lover. This ache you feel is our beautiful humanness. You can call it many things... love sorrow joy longing. it really has no name. without it how would we know that we are?

you resonate with these songs these words because you know deep down that they are your beautiful reflection. when you hear your heart song it is undeniable. you follow the music as these are the most beautiful wondrous words you have ever heard. they ache they pierce you deeply touching you in secret places that you did not even know existed, revealing a magic you just knew must be here. yet you could not even dream of this wondrousness as it is far beyond imagination or belief. it is the living pulsating aliveness, this unadorned vibrant beauty of life streaming though you as you, raw and naked marvelous beyond measure, and yet revealing the magnificence of the worded world of the color red, of tears. And salty sweetness of the merging of joy and sorrow of life bittersweet bursting in echoed grandeur mutipetaled flowering flowing dream scapes streaming dancing shimmering shadows into love and love lost blossom and a return to marvelous quiescence, that all consuming ever subsuming liquidity of home

And tendrils of emptiness untie themselves and reveal the flowing jewel that had sparkled so. Reflected in your lovers eyes in the wetness that slid in between. In sidewalk's echoes of all your dreams forever shattered, And never sought again

The brilliance was always on, but seeking it cast a shadow. For what you are is unseen but felt fully Nothing other can be found. Breath weeps words soundlessly into songs of utter beauty. Words create this imaginary separation, And words flow around and through the space in between, We need em to exist and love, Yet when we can no longer find ourselves we slip silently into and through each other We are but fictional choice-less characters dancing in a mirage

turquoise bottom clouds sail across sky kissed seas spilling midnight blue inky shadows into seamless waters this dancing falling fleeting streaming sailing tumbling flowing precious immediacy life kissing itself through the unique lens of you... snowflakes melting into themselves... feels like beauty and love and wonder. To know that we know the preciousness of knowing is the greatest gift of all. Self a beautiful transparent lens through which the universe catches a glimpse of its own beauty and majesty. only through us love and beauty enter the universe

I swim in the seamless sea of utter beauty... sometimes my feet touch the sandy bottom and I speak with friends... my heart aches with their splendor...I gaze in awe at this magnificent world...centerless edgeless measureless... I am smitten with the absence of meaning... the dropping away of hope and fear and any concern with the outcome.. I stretch my fingers into the sky and the universe swallows me...I stretch my toes into the groundless earth and they find no hardness or softness...I open my hand and find...nothing... and my hand disappears

at first it's like you are standing on the banks of a mighty river, and you fling out your net sparkling in the sun and watch as it lands in the water... and are disappointed when it comes up without any water...you are terrified of getting wet...yet you are drowning with thirst...

...then one magical day you simply slip down the banks...your longing for water has overcome your fear of falling...
....and you realize all of a sudden that words and thoughts are not supposed to catch or stop or divide the river in any way.... and you are not even on the banks or the caster of the net...
....you are the river and the river is you.... and the net is not supposed to catch the river... simply part of the show....

we are the voices we hear
we are the song
the singing
the lover
the love

we are lost as love
In love
Alone
together

we soar in as utter this beauty of a shoreless ocean, we play in pools of love as rainbows reflecting on the surface reflect back on the sandy fathomless depths... no directions are found or lost... seamlessly dancing in our own starlight. There is no cause for concern it is not your dance, its only dancing. sunlight scattered waves endless vault of sky slips through fathomless depths shadow-less shadows dancing. Deep. Sublime. Peace

EARLY AUTUMN SONGS

It appears to others that I'm walking talking, feeling and acting yet my lips kiss, my mouth sings all by itself. I have no concern to discover where the music comes from or why, as truly, it feels like I am an empty shadow dancing in and as and through a brilliant ephemeral dream. Simultaneously amorphous, yet with rhythms, and wordless, yet with lines spoken by no one by everyone.

Some make believe characters believe they are the singers and others know that there is no singer no dancer no actor no rhythm no rhyme, and all of us swooning into the unheard music never ending always ending, never beginning always beginning, as time lost its footsteps long ago in this dream that danced its way into a silhouette of me.

Colored by ancient shadows, illuminated by primordial vibrations that were never separate or joined, there are no separate moments or notes yet songs fill the darkness of our hearts written on a ribbon that sometimes feels like a message wrapped up in tears or smiles or deep deep despair or joy. Nothing need be done to hear the message to unfurl the paper of the paper cup that is your heart. It can feel like love and joy to know that there are no borders except these imaginary lines that paint themselves yet have never captured anything or nothing. Yet it can feel unspeakably melancholy to know there is nothing in the marrow of the drink you drink deeply always.

It seems that most of the day this character called Nancy is walking and talking in and as sublime awe. Vacant wonder fills her shadow until it surges into song. Yet she knows she is not the singer or dancer, that there are no singers or dancers or lovers, simply love streaming through the dream looking and feeling like anything at all. It feels like a continual falling in love as love through love.

Everyone has a feeling that there is magic somewhere, sometimes felt, sometimes missed. Some look for it avidly. I did! Hanging out in nature. Looking for love. Meditation or drugs or books or travel...
Seems often I was just trying to avoid that feeling of somethings missing

Gazing at the featureless ocean
The mind of this and that has no where to cling
Watching a sunset

That
brief moment when the mind is not comparing it to other sunsets
Like falling in love
No reasons are looked for

And all trying to find it
To pinpoint it
To stop it to catch it
To put it in your pocket
To name it

Create the feeling that it is an it, and you are an it separate from it. This cannot be spoken of, this feeling of a hush a pause. Simultaneously an inbreath and an exhale. You know it's there when it feels like you have let go of the handlebars of your bicycle. Yet, you find you cannot let go of this seeking, even though you try to stop trying

Some words or actions may seem to take you to this magic you long for, reading books or being with another or meditation. But the feeling is fleeting, and seemingly contrived. It will not stop your hunger for other better more or next. All action that seems to create the magic perpetuates the idea that your hands are on the handlebars. The tension of the longing to let go and knowing you cannot, the seeking to end the seeking may just rip you apart, eviscerate you, pull out your heart that you were trying so hard to keep

no words can capture it, as all words are things. Lassos around a bit a bite of life, But life is fluid and has no edges, it has no separate moments or things. All seeming separation is created by the thought stream. thoughts words ideas concepts paint the dream of things. There is no escape from the dream of things, as we are made up things also. Fleeting swirling description. We are water colored thought dreams painted on a river. We are made up. The knowing feeling that all the lines are imaginary... That whoosh... That feeling of edgeless super complete perfection. Is the magic that you feel. Yet the tension of trying to capture it, to name it seems to obscure it.

You are the dream of separation. There is no escape coyote. As being in it or out of it is the dream. It's thought words ideas concepts all the way down. ALL this and that is made up. Just like us.

Night winds caressed his face
he heard the crescent moon beckon and like a cup spilled his questions into the sea
with his pockets emptied
Of even moonlight

Silence doesn't exist until named. All words seem to capture a bit a bite of what's going on and create a thing. Even nothing is a thing. Oneness is a thing when named. We are things existing in a world of things, and all this imaginary separation is the dream created by thought words ideas concepts. We cannot escape the dream. We are it.

Every name creates what's in the lasso and what's not. All words are judged as me or not me, and usually judged as helpful or harmful to the self. When the dream of names is believed it hurts.
Silence most often refers to the absence of sound, So that's an imaginary division, creating a razor that cuts. Nothing refers to the opposite of everything. Silence as I refer to it is always on. There is no word for all without edges. I can say it's unspeakable. Yet that implies that there are some things which are speakable. All words weave the dream... Like...This

There exists both simultaneously the dream and that which cannot be caught by thought. They are not two. Or one, or none,

Calling it a mystery is simply another handhold another imaginary reference point in the dream. Seemingly making what's going on understandable, and continuing the illusion of something to understand, and someone to understand it.

The scent of mountain rains blossomed in her heart as she wandered the desert dream trying to slake her raging thirst in every shimmering mirage. The longing to hear the symphony of long lost nights, and forgotten kisses, and the meadowlark's call she almost captured as it tremulously echoed across the autumn fields burned her heart with an indescribable exquisite melancholy, for love for love lost for all lovers everywhere.

Whispers beckoned rippling in the long grasses as they sang of what no words could kiss in tongues of wild undulating rivers of song and silence.

Torrential rains flood the dream and etch away at all sides of empty promises of tomorrow. She leaned back her head and howled at the sky, at the moon, at the sun for this hole that could not be filled, this sublime limitless all encompassing aloneness that had no center or edge. There was never anyone any heart to fill or empty.

And the desert winds picked up her shadow... dancing

Awakening is not like getting a shiny new toy, It's not an attainment or a present. Or about living in the present. Or living or thinking or feeling any particular way. Or about arriving somewhere else like a place of wholeness or oneness. Or understanding. It is not about becoming a better person, or ridding yourself of yourself or your beautiful human-ness. It's not about escaping the dream. t is merely the recognition by the brain that all separation, All separate things and events, Are it's own fabrication. Made up.

The continual anxiety and fear that accompany the belief in a separate person with personal volition who is traveling a razor like timeline from birth to death disappear, and the simple joy and ease of being is always on as awareness finds itself suspended as a sublime edgelessness, an infinite dimensionless edgeless flowing scintillating light fabric, nakedly seeing as if for the first time... a childlike awe saturates the dream that has exploded from the tight confines of I am into an all encompassing flood of we are.

The universe cries out
In the breath between the lips and the song
We appear

and reverberations of timelessness hang in the air like a silent sonic boom and merge into the vortex of the ever emerging ever disappearing now

memories dance lightly with ghosts of the future and are only noticed when someone asks me to dance
and a falling leaf is like a kiss from a stranger
gnarled ancient trees grown and fallen
their wind twisted branches like desert driftwood
countless stories can be written on water about these things yet their utter sweetness is revealed in their dissolving into the river
and endless poems like cottony seeds sail by on canyon breezes backlit by afternoon sun sliding effortlessly, directionless, not caring where or whether they will land
so too how effortlessly life arises timelessly and simultaneously self releases
and no longer looking for what this life is

the utter meaninglessness of even meaningless is astounding
I swoon into the eyes of a passerby

Always felt this delicious softness the knowing feeling of seamlessness
Yet the apparent seams written in the worded world create a forest of dreams where I
waltz through the clearings and under the boughs of beauty that reached into the vast-
ness where my sings unfurl

and wind flies through my hair and I dance with the wind and I am inseparable from all
and everything this rush! of life unowned
tears stream uncaused flying flowing rivers of nothing of everything into
Transparent images that ripple and sing of the wonder of iridescence flowing

Our stories write themselves
simultaneously the words and letters disappear into the vastness
weaving and unweaving a diaphanous tapestry where we are a centerless jewel spinning
radiance

Enlightenment is like being in a movie and knowing it is a movie at the same time.
Knowing you are and all other characters as well as all thingness is dreamt, yet living and
loving as a beautiful imaginary character. There is knowing that there is no waking up
from this dream however, only to the dream. Knowing this shared dream of separation is
the only place you exist. Knowing it is a dream it is simultaneously dreamlike, Impersonal,
yet more vibrant and alive than before, as there is no more hope or fear or need of
next. There is no longer that constant urge to do something anything. As it never feels
like there is anyone doing life. Nor does it feel like life is happening to a someone. The
momentum of a lifetime disappears. No longer constantly trying to find your place on a
timeline a tightrope of hope and fear with death at the end.

It is like a hyper awareness of being aware through this streaming dream of separation,
more lush and rich more miraculous than you could have ever believed or imagined. This
unspeakable awe and sublime ease is always on and can never be kissed with words. It is
known that there never was a self or time or a mountain, Yet we can go walking in the hills
astounded by the unbearable beauty. Isn't it amazing that as you read these words the
images the concept of a mountain appears. Perhaps you can feel the sun and soft wind
on your beautiful cheeks...
The brain uses shared learned words to describe what's going on and creates the story
of this and that and you and me, a passion play with an imaginary self at the center of

this swirling of words thoughts memories…. it can really feel like that that there is a lonely isolated individual separate and apart from the rest what's going on. Because as soon as imaginary separation is born then, well, if there's a thought there has to be a thinker, and if there's a feeling well then there has to be someone who feels the feelings, and if there is perception then there has to be an observer.

When in actuality there are no separate thoughts or feelings or things, here is no this or that until described. somehow the brain which is created this dream of separation this pseudo-reality this virtual reality this magicians tale seems to believes that there is a universe of separate things and separate moments, in time and dimension and measurement. It is quite easy to see that once thought ceases just for a moment all things and you disappear.

So this shift in perspective called awakening which can happen slowly overtime or perhaps all at once is simply the brain not believing in the story that it is painting. As these imaginary lines are seen and felt to be made up sometimes it feels like the boundary between inside and outside is dissolving. Perhaps it may feel sometimes like you are everything and maybe sometimes it feels like you are nothing as you can't find yourself anymore

As self is beliefs as these beliefs are beginning to be not believe there's a feeling of weightlessness sometimes there can be terror. As the world as you've known it and you as you've known it are starting to crash the house of cards the Sandcastle begins to dissolve as the waters of this clear seeing is penetrating this wall of beliefs that seemed to separate a you from the rest of what's going on. Sometimes there can be a feeling of seamless ease that is so wondrous, no longer caring to try to find a place to land and other times it can be feeling like you're falling and there's a feeling of impending doom because it's true your whole life is crashing.

Perhaps there may be a huge feeling of heartache like your morning your own Death, There may be Oceans of tears or spending nights gripped by unseen terrors like you're lying on a bed of nails. Perhaps you may notice one belief at a time suddenly not believed, or perhaps a whole swathe of them seems to disappear and you say 'wow! I don't Believe that anymore!'

And as self is beliefs, well, then there is a dissolution of the belief in self, of the person you thought you were as all ideas of what you are and what your world is like all ideas of what you should be and all ideas of what the world should be like start to collapse. This feeling of homelessness and placelessness can seem wondrous or it can seem scary or both at the same time. Perhaps you start to realize there is no right or wrong way to feel and you start to realize that you were not the thinker of your thoughts you are not the feeler of your feelings, there are simply feelings, there are simply thoughts, It may begin to dawn that there are not separate thoughts or feelings. It might be nice to know that there are other people who have gone through this. Although truly you go through it alone. And you fall until the falling is falling... Awakening is not a walk in the park.

the dancing continues delicately balanced on the edge of a feather
between love and nothing at all
an empty shadow lit from reflected echoes singing the lives of all who have lived and all who ever will
same words same heartbeat same tears, same love

waves crashing into each other
Swirling seafoam
Clouds kiss the receding waters
As wetness sparkling sinks into the sandy beaches bathed in sunset's glow

Softness falling through softness
A hush flies through itself
An unending sigh
Sighing
in the unspeakable space between Breath and song

Unfound spaces inbetween us melt
They never existed

Time died as hope and fear waltzed into the sunset
no more looking for shadows as the brilliance of seamless ease erased what time forgot

Sometimes the breath of aloneness sails through me spinning trails of yesteryear
dream time waltzing blazing paths to no where gone and a deep sadness of when the dream was believed in

What ever it looks or feels like
All of it a complete confirmation of your beautiful aloveness
Awareness aware of being aware
Nakedly unadorned

Intuited unicity is like love and it's on always
There is no need nor hope nor fear

and just like the sea waves rippling or crashing all arise effortlessly with out any one
doing a thing
and sunlight flows freely and sparkles on all the waves and not one is better or worse
than another
and you are the drowning in your own tears your own love your own delicious humanness
It's so wondrous how everything is included
unicity as an idea seems like a putting together of all things, when really there are none
Without us there is no time no place
no feeling of aliveness

All that we feared comes around and kisses us on the mouth and plunges into the inner-
most core of your being. There is no longer trying to escape our beautiful humanness
The longing is who you are

this freshness of an evening rain, tear drops on my phone
and the clouds paint themselves with evening colors

and after the deluge silence creeps in and fills the space where hope and fear disappeared
and your immense gratitude deepened into awe
and love that is no longer needed is the medium in which all things flow

and rainbows slide across the room as long light filters through crystals hung
feathery shadows dancing as tree tops playing in the winds
night moves in yet there is no time when day leaves
all is hushed in silence though the universe is always singing

this un-utterable ferocious terrifying utterly naked being Ness filled every pore of my
being ripped me inside out
pulled my heart out so that it's beating crushed me
it is the rhythm of life that we share the heartbeat of existence this wondrous love

You or self or me most often refer to the made up character. There really is no word for this
awareness perception, as all words seem to split up what cannot be divided or caught as
it has no edges, the imaginary gap between this and that collapses. Between you and life,
you and me. Everywhere you turn, is like swooning into your own winged beauty. Butterfly

kisses from everywhere and no where, as inside and outside have no meaning, and there is nothing left to divide. You find yourself saying, Unabashedly nakedly, 'I love you'.

This love has no words or anything to defend or capture or know
It is centerless edgeless it flows through you as you
You do not have it
You are it
a wave that fills you empties you pierces you and frees you from all ideas of love
It is everything we longed for and everything we feared

It has no questions and seeks not a place to land
It slides easily into the imaginary places between us and simultaneously frees us from our imaginary barriers

It needs no words yet sings

...and his tears scattered through the known dimensions and reflected his brilliance full yet empty erasing all ideas of whose tears whose love whose pain
future and past collapsed into unutterable beauty

and as long as he could remember he was smitten with sunflowers, he read and studied botany and biochemistry, discovering how they grew, he studied physiology and neurology to discover how he could see and touch them. longing to capture their beauty he would drive to large fields of them and sit with them all day watching their beautiful faces follow the sun.

He grew them and watched as delicate birds would land on them and eat the seeds, and after decades of desire to know them, he realized he could never know what sunflowers were. He could never even know what yellow was, and he realized that it was his longing to capture the magic that he felt so deeply created an imaginary barrier between himself and the sun and painted imaginary lines between the birds and the flowers. Realizing he had never been separate from the magic or life he wept.
The magic was the unfigureoutablity, the uncatchableness, it was never lost, even looking for it had been the magic, yet it could never be held or captured, as he was the magic he had been seeking

What makes most people become seekers is the pain. They may label it as many things but the pain is perceived as being so great there is a attempt to escape the pain, usually associated with being human or the self. I called it the pain of life when it began so horrendously at the age of eight. You look around you know, surely someone has got to know what's going on!

So I suppose when I was not trying to escape the pain by looking for a solution to it, I was escaping it with other means, reading books entertainment travel etc. Looking in psychology philosophy religion.

Or perhaps you feel the pain comes from social reasons and so you're looking for a way to improve the world. So if the fall begins and the beliefs about who you are and about how the world is or about who you were supposed to be and how the world is supposed to be start to go away it starts to feel really really good! So there becomes kind of a goal that there would be nothing left. Yet as beliefs about yourself and the world you labeled bad fall away it is wondrous. I remember when I realized that all beliefs I liked were going to go as well.. how I wept!

It may happen that there is in fact a point where it's reached that there is not even nothing left and you are suspended as nothingness. That never really leaves but what happens is the self comes back much as it was before so it may take a while before they become integrated. Feeling like everything feeling like nothing. Yet there can be a beautiful balance, dancing on the edge of a feather between both worlds, the real and the imaginary. One foot in the flowing and the other foot in the dream.

like a wave or a rainbow or a river or a moment nothing can be captured. Life is ambiguous and no matter how hard we try we cannot hold onto a thought or a moment or grasp a sunset. Every effort to stop this flowing to understand it, to try to figure it out perpetuates the illusion of self and other.

and what lies beyond all imagination and description
all beliefs ideas abstractions all knowing based on this and that?
what is this trembling vibrant aliveness that we all feel?
It can never be captured with words as it is seamless there is no place where it can be grasped, as it is all-encompassing there is nothing that can stand outside of it to grasp it
It is utterly open and measureless nothing can be added to it or taken away
it is perfectly complete always
this unutterable beauty always on yet rarely noticed

Tattered filigree of songs unheard unsung yet felt deeply
Twisting and turning soaring through a sea of dreams

empty shadows glimmering in their own reflections a dance without rhythm or rhyme yet
replete with meaningless patternless patterns soaring through an edgeless sea

and ripples flow across and through each other meeting merging melding and dancing
away again to their own rhythms
our breath
released in one ecstatic swoop creates more ripples sliding over and under them-
selves weaving watery tapestries of reflected rainbows that dissolve into the fathom-
less depths

syncopated heartbeats touching falling through imaginary sides reverberating down wall
less canyons
reds and yellows shimmering a desert mirage as swallows swoop and swirl in fathomless
depths of heights unknown
Beckoning no one to join in the dance of echoes

songs prevail in the desert night
reminding one of sleep
as the hush falls through the hush
where midnight caught a glimpse of morning swimming through a backwards glance

he longed for soundless footsteps as he sang in the boundless sky
and love pierced his heart
and blue fell through the blackness
and his feet dissolved in to the shadowy dance
where love died

She flew through the seas alighting on clouds and watched her tears swimming in sunsets
reflected in echoes dream
Sparkling emptiness danced

The silent crack of lightening between everything and nothing
Splits you forms you fills you empties you

You are never the same
Mauled by your own love

This very aliveness just blows you away

There is a sublime aloneness a profound quiescence thst is always on yet silence is not
needed to recognize it
It is always on

Clouds and mist shroud the canyon in silence
canyon wren's descending notes echo on the naked rock
no longer calling for another to soothe this bittersweet sadness
This longing is what I am

Generally I would say that usually before awakening there is a complete personal
Armageddon when everything that you have believed to be true about yourself and the
world, about how you and the world are, or how they should be, or any ideas about truth
or meaning or any ideas that there is anyone even to have a world, especially all of your
ideas about enlightenment are ripped apart and shredded.

It feels like your skin is being ripped off and you are being eviscerated, all your trying or
trying to not try has simply kept the idea alive that there was a you or something to get.
A place to arrive at or something to attain, yet awakening is realizing not only that there
are no things that all thingness is essentially empty, but also that there is no holder of
things. your own essential emptiness is realized. Here it hurt like hell it hurts so bad that
you don't think that you could ever survive it and in a way, you don't.

And when it is realized that all separation is made up the passion play continues to write
and erase itself the self does not go away, it is simply no longer believed. It is realized
that the self is beliefs and opinions and preferences, and most remain the same after the
shift. There is no more trying to fix the self or others or the world, as it is realized that
nothing was ever broken.

Well if you really cannot find a moment, the beginning and end to a moment, then logi-
cally there are no separate moments and it would follow that there is no before or after
or better or worse or cause and effect. Truly have you ever found a next? Yet people will
say all the time that they have never found a next but they still believe in it. They are the
belief in next, self is the belief in separation, in separate moments, in separate things. the

razor of thought, the razor of words seems to divide what is going on into this and that. and yet nothing is ever actually divided there is no lasso that can capture a bit of this symphony of perception that has no edge nor split or division anywhere.

You are the dream you cannot deny it or surrender to it. All ideas of this and that including accepting or rejecting the dream are the dream weaving itself. The feeling of being separate arises equally and evenly and is recognized simultaneously equally and evenly, just as all perception.

Feeling separate from what is going on may be what is going on. You are not separate from the feeling of being separate are you?

you know life really doesn't feel like anything at all does it, it simply feels like itself.
life doesn't look like anything at all does it, it simply looks like itself
what is going on has no outside to it and therefore no inside, Nothing can be added to it, where would it come from? nothing can be taken away, where would it go?

There is no separate you who can step outside of what is going on and manipulate it or accept it or reject it or surrender to it. So it is obviously super complete or perfect always. Even the feeling that this should not be like this arises totally spontaneously like all perception it arises and is recognized without any effort or non-effort. Self like all separation is like an illusion isn't it.

There maybe the belief that there is a chooser of thought or emotion or action, however deep down there is a deep knowing that this is not the case, and the tension between the belief and this intuited reality is horribly painful.

There are may arise a profound shift in perspective where it is realized beyond a doubt always, that there are there are no separate things nor separate moments. Nor any separate person apart from this seamless stream. All there is is in uninterrupted indivisible symphony of perception and the inseparable simultaneous inseparable recognition of it.

there are no two, there is no edge. All diversity all measurement all this and that are conceptual are conceived, mentally fabricated. Yet this dream of separation is the only place where we exist. Knowing that we are the dream of separation it feels simultaneously dreamlike or impersonal and yet more real than real. Imaginary separation is hell is believed in, and heaven when it is not.

The deeply integrated apprehension that there are no things nor holder of them, That all things and you are essentially empty. Is felt deeply. It's never felt like there's a you doing life or life happening to a you. It's not that you are one with everything, There is no you nor things. It is an entirely different way to experience life. A total shift in perspective, Not a belief or understanding.

The closest the intellect can get is that are all things are interrelated, or interconnected. It can be realized intellectually that there is no time... However when this profound shift in perspective occurs, It is like time dies. There is no longer the belief in other better more or next. It is like a runaway freight train hitting a brick wall. All of the momentum of a lifetime stops. It is like your eyes are licked clean of a lifetime of hope and fear
This shift occurs in the brain it is not something that the character can make happen, As the character, you, are imaginary. As self as a product of thought.

Arising in the thought stream which emanates from the brain composed of shared learned words
You are a mental fabrication, a flowing thought dream.
And as such there is nothing you can or cannot do to make this happen
There is no one or no thing that can step outside of what is going on and change it or manipulate it or add to it or subtract from it or accept it or rejected or surrender to it. There is no outside to what is going on and therefore no inside it is not an it nor a non-it. When the belief in separation dissolves it is like the path collapses the ground collapses and any idea of any kind of goal collapse, And it is truly felt to be a seamless streaming, Without any separate parts or edges, Without any ideas of effort or non-effort. It is obvious always that life does itself. Simply so. And it utterly obvious. That there is never ever awareness without perception and never ever perception without awareness. It is only words which make it seem so. And there is never ever finding an edge to this seamless awareness/perception is there, since there is no outside of it there is no inside, so in actuality it is not an it nor a non-it. It is not a thing nor a non-thing, And if there is no outside to it, well then you cannot be outside of it. It is only words that make it seem like there are separate things at all
Inside and outside, Here and there, You and me.

You are that which you seek, yet it is not what you think you are, and yet it includes it Everything is included, Where else could it possibly be?

Self is the belief in other better more next and that belief creates a feeling of someone separate from what's going on. it doesn't feel right, It hurts, So there is a trying to escape the pain. Substantiating the idea of other better more next. It is the seeking for other that creates the illusion of of other. It is the seeking for more. That creates the illusion of more. It is the looking for wholeness or peace or enlightenment that

46

substantiates the Illusion of separation. It is the seeking for next. That creates the illusion of next. It is the seeking to escape the only world you can ever know, That creates the illusion of outside. And inside. Perpetuates the illusion that there is a key to a door between inside and out
And a path to nowhere
Something to attain
And someone to get it
There is no path
Nor anyone to follow it
There is no mountain
Nor anyone to climb it

When this is realized without a doubt
That there are no things
Nor anyone to know or not know this
The path collapses
The ground collapses
And any idea of a goal collapse

And anyone who says there is a path or method to freedom
Still believes there is someone to be free or not free

As soon as you begin to feel separate you will do anything to feel whole again
singing love songs seems to fill the unbearable aloneness
And yet when all of your dreams of filling this hole in your heart collapse
It's like your heart explodes into everywhere and nowhere
And the emptiness is sublime, and still it sings, silently weeping laughing dancing in between movement and non-movement. A heartbeat ricocheting empty parentheses around a hug for no one

And I am but an empty kiss
Burnt on the pyre of love
A shadow dancing in the dark lit by scattered moonbeams of ash'd reflections
A centerless jewel spinning infinite facets of whispered memories lost as soon as they appear on a horizon where light kisses darkness, Where sound kisses silence, as the river flows through me as me, Wetness pours through wetness, swooning through a swoon.
everywhere I look is unbelievably unbearably indescribably wondrous

beautiful Beyond belief
amazed at my own amazement
I sing

Looking for yourself, looking for purpose, looking for an idea, swirling around looking for what's looking, twirling to catch a glimpse of something solid or stable or fixed creates a spinning that seems to have a center. Yet have you ever found anything at all? Even a thing called nothing or emptiness or awareness? You are the enchantment of belief in knowing in understanding in capturing that which cannot be known. You are the bewitchment of belief in other better more next even though you have never found the morrow or a past.

Beyond your name there is not even nothing. Under the costume of petals falling, of feathers dancing, of cloud castles crumbling, of waves crashing on an endless shore there is not even emptiness as you are an imaginary dream character living and loving in a dream world looking for a path to a non existent edge.

Perhaps the path to nowhere swallows you whole as all ideas of solidity crumble like ocean side cliffs tumbling into the surf. All handholds were just empty clouds that you thought you saw images of people and mountains and tender eyes weeping.

There were simply no things to know and no one to know them. No truth or meaning or purpose and no one to have them.

All ideas of solidity are seen through and your heart breaks wide open, your eyes licked clean of all ideas of hope and fear of unknowing. Feeling this unspeakable magic of existing without substance, what a miracle that you and anything seem to appear!

You are left gobsmacked with unbearable wonder, all your senses flung wide open with a beauty an unending explosion of awe.

She forgot to forget and slipped through her own memories like light pouring through light, simply the taste of life tasting itself. Dreams of yesteryear fell through the morrow and she danced naked in the fresh sprung meadow barefoot. An empty silhouette painted with ashes dipped in rainbow tear'd reflections. The ashes blew away and only an imprint of a leaf shadow traced itself on the sidewalk. And the falling stars illumined her heart weeping

Wind blew her shadowed footsteps
Rustling like leaves in the night
whirling skirts untied
threads undone like tattered remnants of dreams and hopes and fear of the morrow
streaming scattering drops of pearlized moonlight
dripping through the rippling mystery and delight of unknowing of placelessness unfound
nor hidden

As the river washed through it's own wetness
In the darkness she tried to find herself and kissed the flowing

Drinking deeply her own light a sublime melancholy without end or beginning wove her
heart dance into the dream of timeless hellos basking in arabesques of sung unsung
good byes

she was swallowed by midnights desire for light
she fell through the moon hanging by a thread of longing to touch the red hot in the
rainbow's end

yet she was a wisp of sparkling with no substance or design dancing falling arising raining
castles built in mid air
leaving no trace
sadness and joy fell into themselves ..and could not be parted

and the sun shone on her nakedness and island winds soared through her
she was light and wind and the tree tops dancing
lost in his own embrace
kissing her nakedness in skinless skies

her pockets had been ripped inside out and she fell through the silver lining shimmering
with angel dust
and had believed she was a bucket of tears
but the ocean called her to dance in its own shimmering saltiness
drowning in utter wetness her feet dissolved into the sands as they crumbled on the
wandering shore
footless she danced
smitten swooning seamless streaming tumbling timelessly

falling rising merging melting swooning swallowed wholly by wholeness itself
collapsing into yourself and newly emerging always the first and last kiss
wake less waves wonder abounds
shiny sparkling skinless unfathomable transparent being
pattern less patterns form within formlessness
everything from nothing
Nothing as everything
and no longer any concern to grasp what cannot be grasped
all known without being understood
utter peace

Simply this
Nothing other this made up world
Confetti falling swooping sliding in kaleidoscopic patterns never forming or unfurling
never captured or set free
The hand loosed itself on rainbows end and untold riches swallowed the shadows of
many colored coins
ripples splashing through waves that never land nor begin
tears that fall in sorrows grace
a bejeweled iridescence where joy and an immeasurable ache caress its own beauty
shimmering as laughing wetness slides down cheeks of awe

it is an imaginary line describing you ...inside and outside are the dream of you

gazing at your own smile from all sides that have no faces
templates blooming in multifaceted reflections never capturing never seeing what is
nothing more nor less than an echoed glance

all we can see all we can know all we can feel all whom we love

a passion play unlike any other
as there is no other
nothing better or more
than this dance of shimmering shadows playing through this mind stream of this and that
and where this and that fall through the cracks there is not even nothing

yet a magnificence trembles just beyond your grasp
As you are it

as it is aware of itself
through the story
the light
the love
the awe
the joy
the bittersweet taste
of
simply
this

Tripling across the memories where desert sands forgot your footsteps, a phantom bird arises soaring skinless in a naked land. You watch your shadow ripple and swirl and play on the ground as it precedes you. Oceans of tears of everyone's sadness, oceans of joy of everyone's joy
oceans of mirrored raindrops... plashing in rain bowed awe

This emptiness this hole in you heart can be overwhelming as you know deep down it's true the silence the stillness the unspeakable unknowing. It's simultaneously unbearably beautiful
And terrifying
Yet it beckons
Longing to fall
Longing to be held
Truly it is a mourning of all you have loved
Including yourself

And love

When you swallow a glimpse of your own essential emptiness and the emptiness of all things
Neither shadow nor light, neither sound nor silence, Neither here nor there. All absorbed into what has no sides or bottom or space or emptiness

It is simply so utterly crushing
So wondrously breathtaking
So stunning
Your heart implodes explodes into vast pristine pure space as all you thought you were and love bleeds into the dream into a primordial love dance singing like this

Even death weeps at its own exquisite beauty

It is so wondrous that all that I had feared and all that I had tried to avoid
(and actually it wasn't just the things that I considered bad or painful it was a losing of all
things that I had considered desirable......)
For when it was realized that when there was Joy I was Joy, and when there was fear I was
fear, and when there was sorrow I was sorrow, and somehow without any warning it was
all seen as a beautiful flowing of our shared humanness.

Like a gazillion falling stars echoing dancing spiraling pirouetting shimmering dying into
each other's most beautiful reflections
the sea crashed into the sky with the force of a thousand suns dying... and his heart
exploded with a force so immense so painful he was amazed to find himself feeling to the
edges of nothingness and beyond
as the dream dances and whispers in the wonder of its own
delight twirling in ever widening spirals of ecstasy

Without soft cheeks to fall upon and delicate tender wetness of our eyes there are no
tears

The curtains have parted
And there was nothing behind door number two
A hymn of beauty admiring it self
A primordial song, a hush of nothing baying begging longing to kiss The lips of it's own desire

And the knowing. the sublime melancholy of knowing that every moment is its
own kiss. emotion un-named un-signed soars freely. a most beautiful part of the
symphony of perception... rushes roars whispers and sings... it no longer beckons,
or calls you demanding to be heard. As you're not separate from it, As there are
no it's...
stories never quite written no longer read dissolve as they appear, no longer clambering
to be heard, rippling through the air in the waters trickling bubbling whirl pooling down
the canyon, kissing articulating the dream of remembered

Impressions like a gossamer woven light raft shimmering on the sea of dreams
footprints dancing on the edge of time
space pouring into space, never full never empty, yet overflowing

it is far too simple for the mind of this and that... the razor of thought to grasp... it cannot be spoken of or thought about or kissed with words in any way... what is red? what is energy? what is not a what... no picture can capture it as it is fluid and has no reference points whatsoever... it is not an it nor a non it

how can you possibly imagine a thing which has no edges nor outside nor inside nor any split or division anywhere which extends infinitely in every direction without direction? all these words simply paint more dreamstuff on the mirror... a painted rainbow weeps at its own beauty... all separate color sight sound sensation is painted by words... without them there is not even nothing... as nothing is a word...

the flame of your own love and desire overwhelm the fear and the flames lick you into their grasp
burnt on the pyre of your own nakedness the ashes blow away as they simultaneously dissolve and reform
emptiness overflowing as wind as light as life as love... flowing streaming rushing roaring through you as you

trying to hang onto heaven with your nakedness, there is no you separate from the current who can let go, The ocean has no boundaries or non-boundaries. There is no wind separate from the ocean. There is no breath separate from sky
Love sings and silence breathes
Love life death
We are it all simultaneously

Sometimes it is just a look. A touch, A shared sorrow, a shared joy, a shared wonder
Mirrors spinning into the night only dissolved into each other's reflections, we kiss and melt into each other. Oneness swallows twoness. Swallows oneness
Not one
Not two
Not none

Imaginary footsteps echo in the night on boundless avenues... spiraling into sky
ricocheted light and sound and life touching itself
Like endless parentheses extending everywhere and nowhere
A kiss without beginning or end
Forever reaching, forever touching

Never anything other than your very own love
that was never yours

A chorus of endless reverberations sings itself
heard by no one
its own music is felt deeply as it paints itself
Touching itself
Life kissing itself
Two sliding into and through each other
A gasp of awe
one without edges
Sings
Through you

the knowing, the sublime melancholy of knowing that every moment is its own kiss
The taste of your beauty shimmers as my own reflection
Only through you do my lips sing of kisses in the fathomless depths where even beauty
lost her grasp on her mirror
The words I love you Are never sufficient
Yet they flow and pierce deeply in unfindable places and radiate outward into unutterable joy

And even in the touchless touch Love songs still emerge of longing to touch to sing to
kiss your very own heartbeat
Your very own love
The rippled vastness
Of wake-less waves
A pulsating
A surging
An ever peaking aria swallowing itself as loves delight

Shadow'd memories of touchless love embraced her heart from the inside and out
and even light does not know what happens in this infinite intimate embrace of love
touching itself
as the hands open and dissolve we become light and love and life itself
weeping at our own beauty

spaciousness consumes all and everything... then swallows itself
and uncountable stars begin to shine

Does the undermutter change after the shift... well the brain must constantly describe whats going on... telling your story... or you and all thingness simply disappear
There is definitely not the constant self judgement and self correction... the momentum of fear and hopeful thoughts... still plans are made

I am flying to Florida Tuesday to spend a week with my Dad
There is not the constant regret singing about the past... the coulda shoulda wouldas
There is not the constant "How am I feeling... what am I feeling
why am I feeling this way... how can I keep or change or manipulate my thoughts and emotions or actions, or how can I change or fix others or the world?"... no trying to figure out why or caring why others or myself do or do not do... as I no longer see people as choosers or actors
Thought continues to paint and erase the passion play, but there is no concern to grasp it or change it
I was noticing this as someone asked, after he asked my how I was feeling, and I was simply stumped

if what I sing of were explainable or teachable or transmittable it would not be it, as it cannot be captured... and that is its beauty. Unbearably wondrous... superb beyond measure
so simple... it cannot be grasped or even thought about
it is who you are
it seems to long to express itself still
I cannot imagine not singing
I love the dance
so poignant... if my heart is not being pierced I cannot find myself
tears flowing through tears... wetness through wetness... light through light... vibrant aliveness kissing itself
through this song as it sings us

kissing the surface the light rippled gently over his lips
hello goodbye hello

a cloud seems like a landmark in a storm, but your feet find no purchase on the reflections from yesteryear, and you can no longer find your shadow, as your story has unfolded into the vastness of all stories
a single tear
wet like wetness
a drop of rain slides into the sea never not wet

This Glistening tender wetness of our beautiful shared humanness
Unwritten stories write themselves. Dancing footless as starlight's echo bathed in the warmth of the moon's reflection. Spinning in the spin of what she no longer cared to catch. Her rainbow skirts fell into the sky

Trailing into infinitely cascading filigreed wonder kissing all and everything into a stream of delight, a timeless ease the backbeat of this unwritten symphony whispering baseless overtones, a wordless wonder sings...

She was a hologram of an endless bow on a package sent to no one, twisting and curling exploding chrysanthemum ribbon, and the empty box, bereft of wishes and dreams was the prize, the present unwrapped itself and revealed gifts beyond imagination
the shock of recognition. The Zing of what can not be captured, the brilliance of seamless transparency, less than a glance. From the side of a rearview mirror. simply so. Revealing itself spontaneously, singing itself as it immediately falls into its own hush...

The paint had fallen off the glass and the light and love she had longed for pierced her and shattered her and scattered her tears like infinitely faceted gems throughout all and everything
and everywhere she looked she saw her own starlight dancing
And everything she touched she felt her own warm tears
she was the scent of scent
the taste of taste
the blue of blue
the touch of touch
More intimate than her tongue in her mouth
an unbearable joy knowing that she was unknowable flooded through her night and day
she wept

There is no concern to capture the light. It is obvious that it's everywhere like a centerless jewel, you are the reflections dancing, streaming light streaming space, streaming stories across the universe
a shooting star in all its glory has no comparison to you

They cast their reflections out to see ...and lit up the ocean
Where day turned to night
The sky tasted moonglow on an empty horizon
Islands merged into bottomless depths and sang of colors dancing in the sands,
Swimming in its own sea of delight, songs of midnight dances rained through nautilus chambers
echoing a dream world that drew her in, nuzzled sweetly she discovered her own kiss
fingers tingling... mechanically move on the screen and filter out bits of nothing that sing

Reflected love caught in the waves, blowing through each other, disappearing into echoed reflections, Songs pouring through the canyon lightly skimming rippling tears
The ebb and flow of unseen tides her heartbeat
Felt deeply desert winds could not be seen
Simply beautifully Vibrant aliveness touching itself

so stunningly beautiful... watching the dance dance itself... knowing you are the watcher and the dance... the lover the loved and the beloved

we are the wet and the water and the flowing... the taste of sweet saltiness as tears slide down your precious tender cheeks... without your delicate vulnerable I's.... there is no kiss of life to touch the wetness. ripples apparently divide the shimmering into separate parts and places in an edgeless flowing... and the weaving cannot be undone by creating more beautiful ripples

She lost herself in the dance... whose arms... whose legs... whose footsteps.. where is where... when is when... whose tears whose words whose love

night swam into the day time dream in a waltz without time or rhythm or words... yet she heard it felt it deeply... it sang of the magic that she was... but had only glimpsed... and she thought she had lost it trying to count the stars... but it was only her breath her tears her love for the enormity of all this... fleeting touching singing.... life kissing itself the dance dancing itself... through her... suspended between nothing and everything... emptiness overflowing only when there are imaginary boundaries can two touch... and fall through them

And traffic roars on mainstreet yet the dancing never stops. We sing as we do no longer looking for the backbeat of time or a place to lay our soft cheek on the darkness

Treasure abounds love lies fleeting, never captured never gained never lost never needing to forget or remember. placidity among the waves of darkness reflecting the ever present fall into sunset's gaze

And the songs write themselves out of dreamstuff and dance on a lonely spider web in the corner of an abandoned boat falling apart in the harbor waves lapping silently paint has been forgotten raw wood softened ropes untied sails.... abandoned
Winds
ever present on a rudderless ship on a sea of dreams

and the strains of last night's love songs rain upon the beach where the rake of morning has not touched
turning stands of seaweed into musical staves where each note is a memory written on the blankness of night time, yet the waves crashing are never lost and the sea breeze turns your hair into curls
reflecting in the moon
rising

And sand and sea speak volumes of waves lost and found and never touching anything other than the song of themselves
Salty sea dreams where sun bleaches out the colors of yesteryear
And the taste is ever sweet

No longer looking to dye the moon blue to erase your own sadness, Your own brilliance reflects on midnight puddles where every tear finds ripples in it's own wake reflecting it's own dream

Only the headlights from afar could show the details in a rock wall, only your own tears could ever reflect the shining love escaping your shadow

Dripping with moonlight the eastern star appears, dancing in shadowy breaks where your blood pooled in its own sadness. And every word hidden until the bottle breaks and the elixir of love is known to be drunk on itself

The hint of daybreak catches your breath with a song that has been on the tip of your tongue since before memory erased it as you dissolve into yourself, wet with your own tears where love never died, it merely was forgotten...

In the depths of the dragon's lair a treasure gleams calling you to pluck it, yet it can never be touched with your own hand, only your fingertips that do not long for treasure can sob

emaciated cloven hooves trot on the boulevard of sadness and write memories in the sand tracing a map of nothing into your brain tying lines of space into knots that can never be undone

Only a reflected sunrise could ever find a magnet to your heart and glue itself to a key that had been lost for a zillion years, yet... it was never lost
the key to your heart
your heart has always been open it was just the music that you felt like a drum in your gut that wrenched the key from your hand and dropped it in the basement of your heart gleaming in starlight it was always here
but never seen
in the puddle of your own tears
Reaching out for love and Touching your own fingertips always wet with your own tears

The brain naturally searches for patterns, But can get stuck on a loop without end
if only the stars really fell on that night they fell in love
She could no longer remember what she wished for. Or why

Pennies in the fountain sparkled just so as the ripples covered them and revealed them they seemed to swim as watery dreams of promises unkept
The universe had no rhymes that would reveal its secret path to love
Hopscotching down the path she arrived at an overgrown woods.... it seemed the answers lay in the tangles but she could not unravel them without breaking them
and her tears fell in the moist earth as she lay under the brambles
Under the falling sky

the pony pauses... at the edge of the meadow... Smelling the lightening on the mountain he starts to dance. And wild eye'd mountains laugh singing tales of cougars high up in the rocky cliffs as every single hair registered the winds
and the wind blew through him as he was the wind falling into and through itself life folding crashing into unfindable unbearable magnificence
the young colt could smell the storm
and lightening filled his being... fire on the mountain

as the wind rippled through the long grasses
touching him
piercing him
with his own beauty

catching dancing sunlight in his heart
the sky swallowed him as he ran naked through vast spaciousness
the rawness of life cut through to the marrow of his being
soaring skinless... through a river of dreams
every sensation every sight sound feeling... mirroring his utter delight

trembling tenuous Uncapturable radiance ...flowing streaming tumbling mountain brook
laughing throwing priceless iridescent gems into the air as it longs for the deep blue sea
And the sunset colors illuminated every grain of sand beneath his feet has his footsteps
filled with tears and crumbled under the weight of his own desire

Everything that I wanted to avoid or run away from has become so marvelous so sublime
so heart achingly wondrous. All I see is beauty unowned. There is truly nothing here. No
here nor there

I bask in your sunset. I cannot see myself

That deep deep emptiness you feel inside sometimes, that hole in your heart aches to
be filled..
You hear it and yet there's something intriguing in it, there's something that calls you. A
longing to fall into nothingness and a long longing to be held at the same time... There can
be a great fear, the mother of all fears, of falling deeply truly in love. As you lose yourself

And yet birds fly across sky like vastness and never look for a trace that cannot be found.
Of where they have been, Or why

And why should you be afraid of nothing
And why should you want it so

how the birds sing on this winters eve, plashing in our fountains we keep filled. how lovely
this vast spaciousness without beginning or end or time. How sublime the fullness. Of
you and me and love and beauty

One can live beautifully suspended knowing that there are no things and that they are marvelous mentally fabricated dream stuff. Living. Dancing on the edge of a feather. Between love and nothing at all

Obviously any organism will try to avoid or get away from physical pain, But only the human brain objectifies the stream of perceptual input, Calling it perception, And believing its a thing. Creating the belief in an observer. Calling the flow of perception sight, Sound, Touch, Taste, Sensation
Creating the belief in a separate listener, Toucher, Feeler, Taster
And feelings are labeled joy, Sorrow, Love, Despair, Anger, Excitement, Fear
And are judged as good or bad

And just like physical pain and pleasure, The imaginary feeler of these feelings, self, Tries to hold onto or get away from them
Or perhaps has learned that if he just lets it go, Or accepts it or surrenders to it, It will somehow mitigate the pain

Same with thoughts. The labeling them as thoughts. Creates the belief in a thinker, and some labeled bad or good. And around we spin... Trying to create good thoughts good feelings. there is nothing wrong or right with this, It's perfectly natural
Yet it is painful as it perpetuates the painful illusion of a you separate from thought or feeling
ALL perception occurs spontaneously and naturally. Simultaneously self arising and self releasing. Thought seemingly creates separate solid things, But there are none. Just a flowing water color dreamscape painted on a river. So beautiful. So wondrous. Just like you

Self is
You are
The brains beliefs and preferences
So you do not prefer to feel sad
Or feel or think certain things
It feels wrong
And you want to change them or avoid them
And perhaps it feels like you can
Because it's never the same thought or feeling, Yet there are no separate thoughts or feelings

Life may seem like an endless card game of constantly judging and trying to rearrange what's going on, yet It's ALWAYS what's going on. Isn't it

And where did you get the idea that certain thoughts or feelings were wrong?

All thought all feeling all perception arises spontaneously and quite naturally. Evenly and equally. Without any effort or non effort. And is simultaneously and inseparably recognized. It is the same this flow of perception and the recognition of it. And perception is judged as helpful or harmful to the body and self. Sometimes the judging is judged. And ALL THAT happens all by itself. Utterly naturally. Life happens all by itself, and looks and feels like anything at all

You are not the do-er of life, or the chooser of thought feeling action. If it feels like you are can you choose to stop feeling like the chooser?

There are no wrong or right feelings or thoughts and no chooser of them, and no separate thoughts or feelings. No wrong or right way to live. Or love. Or die
This is it coyote

Until the perceptual input seems to be lassoed and put into boxes of this and that there is simply an indescribable unknowable unknown without color or shape or any qualities or characteristics at all
You can't even say it is fluid because that would imply that there is something solid or permanent
You can't even say that it is edgeless because that would imply something that could have edges
We exist only as these magnificent dream characters in this wondrous dream world and there's no escape from the dream as there is not even nothing outside it
..there is no outside to the dream
inside and outside like all this and that are dream words dream stuff
And the dream crochets itself just like this, simultaneously self arising and self releasing. All by itself
And it simply looks and feels like anything at all

Like a vague whisper in your dreams
A song you just knew you had sung

Once
Long ago
But had never heard
Of a time and place that had no time
Or place

Of a kiss
That had no inside
Nor out

Of a wind
That sang
Your name
But wasn't yours

Of a wind
That caressed
A part of you
That was
Wind
Itself

Of a love
Centerless
That loved you
Without boundaries

And a lifetime of trying to remember
The words to a song
That had no words

Of trying to catch a melody
That had no time

Of trying to reach deep inside for a place that was never hidden
Nor lost

Nor found

Like searching forever in the dark for light

And finding
That all your shattered dreams
That pierced your heart with longing
Were ice crystals
In the summer sun

And butterflies hovered in empty footsteps
And tears filled the cracks that time forgot

And dream shadows danced
With moon light streaming on the sidewalk

Not even the faint smell of the spring rain
Not even the reflection of starlight in a puddle
Not even the echo of geese returning north
Not even awareness
Nor beingness
Nor even suchness.
Not nothing
Nor anything
Beyond this or that
Or when
Or how
Or why

And you exist as memories of someone you knew long ago blow across the great divide
Whispering footfalls that crumbled under the weight of oceans of tears
An echo Dances lit from shimmering mirrors
Vast spaciousness has lost its name but turns around and kisses you
I disappear into the crochet the sun the cat the sounds of the birds
Sparrows Robbins woodpeckers and my husband silently sitting

and innumerable stories flow through this mindstream painting an etch a sketch outline
of footprints in the wind

how beautifully fleeting this glance of butterfly kisses reflected in moon glow
enamored with their own refection sometimes they drown trying to catch a glimpse of
themselves with beating hearts and wings

the scent of lightening rushes through the meadow and long grasses sing your name
imprinted in your heart a desire to sing
rich and lush beyond measure a fantastical flowing thought dream colors in a dream
through the prism of your kiss
like a song you long to hear but cannot remember a whisper of a touch that burned kisses
into your heart it was never my love that opened your heart

hearts opening... tears at what we thought was someone else's pain
a most beautiful ripping ,,of hearts
unabashedly beautifully human
wrapped in our own infinite intimate embrace
an unending stream of perfection of super completeness

a chorus of winds streams flows through you and sings
simply tears reflecting your beauty like ripples in the thought stream bathing in the unde-
niable wondrousness of what ever seems to appear

she peeked into a hidden corner of her heart
where walls of fear kept her from falling
out into the moonlight
sparkling on the waves
sucking the sand
and rocks
and her reflection
into the sea

the incredible journey no one took
no one arrived
nothing was left
even the emptiness
fell out

INDIAN SUMMER SONGS

and there are curtains flying in the wind rippling names of far away places where you will one day arrive and slough off your beautiful humanness... singing songs of evermore or nevermore... of castles in the sky... of cloud free days and the end of storms and the last sunset which seems to always beckon... this will be the end of you the sage sings, yet she seems to be sitting across the table from you smiling and crying and toasting the end of the day

what is under a cloud shadow, can you pick up the darkness and see are there pockets in your heart?where love is hidden? can you slide on starlight as it bathes the dream of night? can you waltz in a rainbow as it falls into sky...

and all your dreams of love and forever and enlightenment are like ships that have lost their sails as you feel the very wind take away your last breath as you feel all the love you longed for take away your heart

and no one can sing of this utter devastation how you have been ripped to shreds eviscerated by your own love that no guru could give you nor take away... under your dancing shadow there was not even nothing... under the dream of love not even a tear... yet tears still flow as this unutterable majesty what you call life continues to pour though you as you unbound emptiness fills you empties you

an empty glass holding more than you could have ever wished for... drinking deeply the stars shine through you, and throw waves upon the sand where you walk breathless... shadowless footfalls sink in this fathomless sea that you are, drenched in salty tears... your heart weeps and reminds you that yes you remain.... loving so deeply this brief brief window of life tasting itself through your tears

You are this delicious liquidity of home... sublimely bittersweet oceans of tears have called you yet you have never left, it was love falling into and through itself. A constant kiss a constant union of what was never apart... everywhere and nowhere this all encompassing supersaturated infinite infinite embrace. Flowing out, flowing in, the universe breathes and sings your name... dancing you are the dance. singing you are the song. loving, you are the love the lover and the beloved... you reach out your hand to touch the beauty that is everywhere and your fingers are drenched in your own tears... you cannot turn away from this unbearable magnificence. For it is you... never ending never beginning always ending always beginning... A brief brief window opens through your eyes and life falls in love with itself... the universe blooms into oceans of petals through your lips... through your song shine and shade ripple overtones vibrate and fill your sails with a contrapuntal madness that races through your heart and bursts through the imaginary line between sea and sky between you and me

love and sorrow shimmer across the sea of dreams of never and forever where your ship lost its keel and all wishes for safe harbor blew away in the tempest that lost even tomorrow... you cannot look behind for everywhere you turn your shadow dances and all dreams of union were dashed on this shore-less ocean when there were no hands nor hearts to join no footfalls left an imprint on this trackless land as their sides crumbled in the dust of your tears... stories left empty pages strewn like haphazard stars across the night never joined nor separate simply light streaming through you as you

tears cast their watery glance across your starlit cheeks reflecting their primordial hum in your smile and you cannot find yourself without their reverberations ricocheting through another's eyes swooning into and through your own echo you are the bittersweet heart ache of aloneness dancing a dance with a necklace of skulls ravishingly heart achingly devastatingly beautiful... this life this life this unowned life stunningly amazing rippling roaring streaming soaring love dances as this infinite sea of dreams... Nothing but your own lips kissing themselves. Sky kissing sky

How can I describe this vast spacious seamlessness that fills me empties me pours through me and writes these lines I cannot point to what has no center or edges or sub-stance at all? How can I point to something which has no separate parts which has no split or division anywhere? How can someone point to a thing which is not a thing or non thing? Nothing cannot be pointed to as all words paint the dream. How can you point to nothing? A spaceless space without edges or center or direction or time or dimensional-ity or measurement? Emptier than empty

Light falls into light, space falls through space... Emptiness explodes into emptiness... It's like a cup of wine and you drink the wine and then you take off the sides and bottom off the cup and then you pour out the emptiness... wordless wonder surges and explodes into song falling into and through its own rippling shadow... flowing through the sea of unknowing... we are it which is not an it without time or direction or change or perma-nency, flowing without movement... your hand cannot grasp it your tongue cannot speak it your lips cannot kiss it, your heart cannot lose it

What you long for, Ideas of attainment Or arrival Love Peace Enlightenment... All learned ideas... Swirling beliefs about how life or you should be. All ideas centered around an idea of rest.. For the search to stop. All your life you've been on a search a treasure hunt. Always hints of sparkly gems Refracted reflected in a rear view mirror. It wasn't always this painful you scream! This feeling that you or life is not good enough and that it needs fixing. But like a song that you heard once in a dream, A fleeting glimpse of a melody echoed in moonlights glance. You long for that return Of a deeply felt essence that has no name nor non name. If you could only capture it swallow it become it...

You already are it. Underneath the skin The kiss the lips the teeth the bones the heart... Beyond ideas of this and that Here and there You and me Both and neither... A magnificence of indescribable vastness Pure and clear Spaciousness beyond measure. It simply has no name. Not even yours

It is not a thing nor non thing It cannot be pointed to as it has no edges or sides. No inside nor outside. It cannot be grasped by the mind of this and that. It always feels like it is just behind the clouds. it is felt deeply but it is beyond belief or understanding or imagination. words cannot kiss it. As it is not an it or non it. Obvious clearly apparent. It is the attempt to hold the magic that makes it feel like there is a you and it, Separate, And a distance that must be crossed. This pulsating vibrant aliveness Uncapturable Uncontained, Without time or non time... Without a goal what are you? Without an idea of other or more or better or next, what are you? Self is addicted to searching. The seeking defines the self. The seeking keeps you safe Safe from the realization that You are not.

and the lines and squiggles of letters seemed to stretch into gossamer threads of words that could capture a bit of sky, crocheting a piece of blue here, and some clouds there. How could sun and light and love be strung into a bejeweled necklace worn like tumbled shells washed in by the tides? Every word like a needle piercing your heart when the story feels like a battered ship waiting to be blown asunder.. sunset approaches and begins to kiss your inevitable doom and yet your story weaves itself never done nor undone unraveling an untold dream of never and forever

no more looking for peace or love or enlightenment or meaning, no more trying to build scaffolds to reach the stars and fill your heart with moonlight, no longer trying to try to be to feel to think a certain way, there are no more ways. the path to nowhere collapses, the goal of what you knew not vanishes. as you are no longer looking for a place to rest, the ground falls away and silence sings a place-less place of sublime unknowing and embraces the mind in utter rest

Life kissing itself through your tender fragile delicate eyes. Beautiful beautiful you. Sublimely bittersweet this song of love that allows awareness to be aware that it is aware. We are empty reflections of love's shadow

We are Infinite mirrors dancing lit with each others reflection. we are simply made up holograms that exist only in each other's Beautiful beautiful eyes. And Love the best part of the dream, a scintillating centerless Jewel that sings through me with unending tears. we exist only in the imaginary spaces between each other.. and need each other to find ourselves...... we simply do not exist alone and yet we are ultimately sublimely alone. Dancing emptiness swooshing into and through itself marveling at the undeniable simple beauty that can never be kissed with words yet words arise and only through these beautiful stories that we are can we touch

knowing and feeling this utter spaciousness the mind continues to swirl gossamer wing'd thought dreams but there is utter rest that is untouchable. and there is the hush you sought yet it is not a silent mind, it is the exhale of knowing there is no next

Weeping laughing smiling at her own reflection shimmering in her tears wingless soaring flowing as the wind and wind flows through her as life kissing itself. Come hither, she Sang, there is not even nothing I can give you. you are the dream painting itself and knowing that will not stop the tears... How could there be no next he asked? that is thought marking your place in the sky... As it pours through itself washed away in water color dreamscapes

Without this love without these tears how could you find yourself

and the sweetness of emptiness overflowing a birdsong echoes in the canyon coming from everywhere and no where, marvelously unfindable the song describes the vastness the edgeless beauty.. like shadows swirling around shadows words softly kiss what cannot be kissed like a warm breeze caressing your cheek, like the flight of a butterfly describes the space in which it flies... a touch so soft only the memory is felt... clouds reflecting the sun after it has set... remembering a taste of a song you never heard... all trying or trying to not try was like attempting to capture a rippling rainbow in your hand

such a delicious kissing of what was never apart... a sublime unicity in all the myriad explosions of infinite beauty, in the indescribable flow of union, of indivisibility. Love lover and loved together infinitely as steam from my tea cup rises and curls unfurling in the morning sun streaming through my window, the space within the swirling is not separate from the space outside. space only seems to be woven within the dancing, enclosed and then released... so is this life without edges or borders woven into intricate patterns with itself, yet never becoming tangible like a dreaming streaming timeless flowing a dance within a dance... and we are the flowing, our lives bleed into the lines the edges that never have been. we were never separate, we are the dance of the universe touching itself through the prism of our beautiful beautiful eyes

Vast pure sky like spaciousness appeared to shatter into myriad reflections of heart piercing blue, Never mended nor broken... Every imaginary piece an illusion of poems lost in an inescapable dream land streaming crying out its indescribable beauty... words streaming through and around themselves appear to create a substantial reality, this jeweled garment that is you is woven from not even nothing, and is marvelously transparent. the threads the beliefs of who you believe yourself to be unravel and you are skinless utterly naked unadorned, yet the centerless jewel that is you remains as life knowing itself. We are vast edgeless sky bursting into bloom. Rootless boundary-less center less brilliant emptiness

nothing need be found nothing can be lost... there are no things nor a hand to hold them... falling with no place to land until even the falling is falling. The essence of loveliness is this delicious un-knowing and impermanence. Echoed in unseen canyon walls. Felt and never captured. .The magic sings itself, a magnificent chorus of one. heart strings vibrate this and that, singing the heartbeat of existence

Love sings unencumbered. Wondrous beyond measure. The song of the universe plays itself and you arise in the center of the heartland of love. A web of delight drenched with tears woven of unutterable wonder dancing in echoed embrace. secrets unravel themselves in the utter intimacy of love loving itself, life kissing itself in your infinite intimate embrace. It is love which lights the heart lamp of our beautiful humanness and pulls us back from slipping away... One foot in the dream the other pulled into the vastness. Joy and sorrow merge into a sublime bittersweet deep current of unnamed emotion. In the end when there is not even nothing left, You slide into your broken heart. And sing

this unending awe is a most precious jewel this gem of unknowing tugs at my heart like finding my long lost lover everywhere I turn. going nowhere, everywhere is home

and what is it that ripped apart the vines that had entwined your heart that had grown for a lifetime into a wooden pyre of fear aching to be burnt? and what drank that empty space that filled your heart so greedily? jackets of sunset clothed your hope of a new day one warm summers evening as you lay in the grass and dreamed of starlight... how did the stars touch you so? how did they reach down and swallow you in your own naked wonder?

it was not words that untied their own lines and squiggles that had seemed to lasso a piece of sky, it was not that steam from your tea that you lost yourself in, or that canyon that beckoned you by its waltzing slender cottonwood trees gathering their springtime green, or those tender wishes gathering on the doorstep awaiting your next step, or the songs of morning that broke your heart... it was tendrils of your own love that were the fingers that untied the knots that had cradled the story of endless love. you were the story of love songs weeping singing your own demise

after the shift (awakening enlightenment liberation), which does not happen to the imaginary separate character, and seems to happen to a metta program in the brain. (never used that term before yet obviously I have heard metta program from somewhere) as it supersaturates the entire perspective of the character like cleaning the lens of the feeling of being separate, of the feeling of there being separate things separated by space and separate moments divided by time...

and as the virtual reality thought paints continues to constantly appear like a palimpsest within the perceptual input the describing does not stop, still the sage continues to sing of what it is like, still the brain of a sage will continue with an undermutter of shared learned words.

and it is true that we sing of this that cannot be sung of through the lens through the conditioning that we are. and will seem different according to language and culture and what the sage heard and saw before the shift. and will change as she continues to sing

and as self remains after the shift yet looses its relevance, still self is desire. the longing to sing of this to share it even though I know it can never be kissed with words or shared paints my imaginary lines. when I am not singing of this there is simply the feeling of being suspended as awe

And all this is description words flying out of my mouth as if there was a person here who knew something when in actuality there's always a beautiful knowing that it is simply the dream painting itself. Ceaselessly it paints itself, for if thought were to stop then we would not be human. For without the dream of separation awareness could not be aware that it is aware. Oh! Nor love nor beauty nor wonder

And what is it that you long for? What is it that you seek? What awakens you in the deepest hours of the night? What illuminates your dreams? What is the fullness that fills your heart And empties it? What is this life That slays you with its unbearable beauty and emptiness?

Can you catch it? What would you do with it if you could? How could you separate yourself from that which has no edge? How can a rainbow catch the sky crying? and they danced and danced and no longer cared to find the meaning of the steps of music of love

and your own love pierces you deeply in places you had no clue even existed that frozen chamber of fear begins to thaw you start to unfurl and your heart rips itself out of your chest in infinite radiance as your being is flung across the universe and you see your reflection everywhere...and the little girls dance ringlets down the laughing street bathed in streetlight where your tears have never stopped flowing

and tears like raindrops trace rivulets down the window rainbow gems in early morning light fog drifting apart and merging again, hiding the canyon walls... stories woven from gossamer threads forming the essence of self, constantly changing fleeting fluid edgeless unfindable insubstantial... like ghosts we cannot grasp things our hands fall right through.. we are the dancing itself, and there is nothing outside the flowing as there is no outside... the music rips us apart and drifts right through us

and your song alights on love's radiance as tears pour joy and sorrow through the vacancy left when your heart dropped out of the race as starlight dances laughing at its own footlessness

and I was lost drowning in an ocean of tears... rainbows rippling on the surface reflecting through the weight of light on the rippling white sands below... not being able to discern up from down... panicking... utter release... Drowning... Yet still breathing... Awake adrift on a sea of dreams... Rudderless wakeless iridescent ripples sparkling all around and through me...The crown toppled off and there was really nothing underneath... Not even nothing, not even nakedness...

More marvelous than words could ever touch. Sending kisses to the stars and knowing it is always my own song echoing back resounding through the vastness. Ripped inside out a hollow vessel Overflowing... Dancing easily this sublime madness in the vacuum left when hope and fear flew out the window

Colors have to be separate to weave and unweave themselves into countless unfindable patternless patterns rolling and swirling a danceless dance headless surfing on an edgeless sea. And the fiery orb sails over head drenched in vault of sky and burns a path where time escapes. Pirouetting in mid air sliding down rainbows to catch a kiss of color my heart broke into innumerable pieces and was catapulted into the sky... Loves reflection showered my eyes with my own unnameable beauty pouring through me as me without direction as love kisses itself... through these eyes oceans of loves reflection continue to flow as tears

And loves dreams cast shadow'd nets into pools of echoes that caressed my cheek.. under the song there was no melody nor timbre nor hue Nor color that could catch itself without me to cast it always just beyond my hand my heart... I slipped through the lasso of clouds... As sky sipped sea through a straw and drank deeply this unquenchable thirst filling me emptying me a bottomless empty treasure chest

blueness without end or beginning spun a dream of a dance where I had remembered losing my step but could not catch it or hold it... treasured backwards glimpses sideways glances... chambered nautilus tumbling rushing down the shimmering sands glissading into an edgeless sea

And shadow'd dreamscapes seemed to rise up to kiss an empty horizon where love lost her petaled glimpses of doorways beckoning her across a threshold that time forgot. Whose feet wandered into deep tear'd forests submerged in desert sands? Whose song echoed forth in starlight wonder of days where nights stretched out their wings and embraced tender light kissed shadow as aching hearts spied their reflections... and bled into the dream? And love was a byline an empty space that collapsed into itself as it blossomed into an empty shell and sung sea dreams where loves heart magic told its tale. singing songs of nowhere a melancholy melody without words reaching for the alphabet of the universe bursting into joyous refrain. I am the mist condensing on the inside of this paper cup as it pours empty dreams into a belly of love... a watercolor dreamscape paints a picture of me Swirling into my own embrace

And in the hush of early early a wind sweeps across the night time dream and caresses my whispering kiss into a song where love appears like magic, so we can bask in each other's glow

How can we sing of what has no words? How can we kiss what has no other? How can we touch what we are...

and it was only shades of nothing weaving themselves into her braids that seemed to tie up a shadow... worded signs on a map-less land hiding the buried treasure of her overflowing heart ... and she was just a beautiful story written with rainbow tears on a flowing river as she slid through her empty footfalls on the ocean... amazed at the hugeness of utter emptiness as it hummed her name in every seamless ripple... every sourceless reflection shimmered a love song echoing its own wordless majesty in her sigh, her touch, her glance... and a mirage dances slowly in the heat of midnight wandering in wordless wonder, singing of the ecstasy of being kissed from within

You are a flowing water color thought dream panting itself with butterfly iridescence disappearing as soon as it seems to brush sky like vastness with your empty silhouette... and there is no hand that holds the brush, No scaffolding to hold up the sun, no pocket to hold that rainbow when you lost yourself as it faded in rippling sky... clouds forming and dissolving simultaneously, they look like anything at all... and nothing bows to your scintillating shadow as you dance through long summer grasses dipped in starlight

and where is your reflection in the wind, sighs the tree tops as they dance with no plan or rehearsal. you looked but could not find it, it was only the wind stroking your delicate tender heart with dreams of solidity that crumbled under the weight of a thousand tears

The emptiness of which I sing is far more empty than empty. It's not like oh there's a parking space it used to have a car in there and now it's empty. It's not like, oh! there's a glass! I drank all the wine and now it's empty. For that implies a measurable space, and this emptiness has no measurement nor non measurement. It's more like after you drink the wine the sides and the bottom come off and all the emptiness is poured out. Devastatingly ravishingly beautiful. There are no hands that can hold this emptiness. There is no heart that can be filled. there are no secret places where you can hide. all your pockets ripped inside out vanished as your hands combed the sky looking for moonbeams... there are no things left to hold and no one to hold them. Most who see through the illusion of self believe they are an unchanging thing called awareness or consciousness. Hanging on to this Idea of solidity. But there is no one to hang on. No one to identify or not. Not even awareness or emptiness...

And you are the ache for other that will somehow fulfill you complete you until it's realized that there were never any separate pieces that needed to be put together. Life has always been indivisible Edgeless Unfathomable. You were never separate. and memories like silvery shadows dart and hide in the bushes, they fade into the evening and leave no trace. like wind's rippling in fields of grasses occasionally they form small dust devils that clear the streets of crushed and tattered litter and it all blows away like a night hawk's flight or that shooting star you once saw blazing an unfindable trail in the darkness, describing an arc with a pin point of light like these words seem to inscribe the vastness with edges and lines that paint themselves like rainbow jewelry in flowing water and do not contain the essence of life but are merely part of the streaming flowing that takes my breath away. Weaving in and out of itself so. Water colored tears slide, Painting your thumbprint on the sky

The stars shone with such brilliant magnificence the imaginary ropes they hung from let loose and they fell into your eyes. Love dances its own sweetness. Drinks its own beauty. Fills you empties you rushes as you. Rips you inside out and twirls you spins you is you...

He was so terrified of naked tears puddling in rainbow pools, shimmering trembling rippling exposed in his lovelight. His tears dripped down his scaredy cat whiskers into his bottomless bowl of love. He finally drank deeply, and Fell into and through his own reflection. His face was etched with smiles and tears, it always seemed to move and dance and hold his beautiful eyes. He was astounded to discover he had never done anything in his life. He ...jusssss ...couldn't get over it life happened all on its own without any effort without anything needing to be done. His whole life he had believed himself to be the captain of an imaginary ship Battling fierce storms. Ship of fools On a sea of tears. And the wind rustled the leaves and sunlight splashed on his tender face.

The flowing the Intense longing the joy the pain the sorrow is who you are this tender beautiful aching heart explodes into everywhere and no where and you can no longer find your lines. There are no words that can catch or hold or kiss or touch or embrace what's going on. Not even the faint smell of the spring rain. Not even the reflection of starlight in a puddle. Not even the echo of geese returning north. Not even awareness. Nor beingness. Nor even suchness. . Not nothing. Nor anything.

As this unknow-ableness has no edges to define it or pocket or place to put your hand into it and grab a part of it, as your hand is what's going on. You are what's going on. You cannot jump outta what's going on, Cause the jumping is what's going on. It embraces subsumes all ideas and definitions of what's going on. The idea that there are separate parts may be what's going on. Or the knowingness of indivisibility. Or believing you are separate and can catch it rearrange it accept it or reject it or allow it or push it or pull it or surrender to it or ride purple unicorns into an everlasting heaven. All What's Going On! No escape! There is no separation. Period.

like the blind we stretch our hands searching for something to touch and the very act of searching is what we are, this inexhaustible search for the light we know we feel must be there somewhere outside of us. It is only the belief in separation which seems to shut out the light. Like an avalanche of concrete it slammed. there was a separate me and the rest of the universe. It was simply a most painful misconception... there were never any separate things or events or meaning or non meaning at all... and out of the inky blackness like a lightening bolt the fullness emerges and rips you to shreds and you get it without having it the preciousness is in the fleetingness and the knowing that life cannot be figured out or captured all other knowing slips away

and the black silhouettes of trees burnt long ago are the background for the new growth bursting in springtime joy. iridescent blue shadows smile through tender green. the transparent crystalline emptiness naked in its supreme brilliance... thought does not obscure this sublime stillness... utterly naked skinless alone moonlight ripples through me ever empty yet overflowing... even the sun is eclipsed by this edgeless beauty... knowing that we know... and the precious jewel of death is always with us...no more lack or needing to know to grasp to capture this fleeting beauty this unfathomable indescribable brilliance... and the wowness of it all consumes me it simply blows me away and I cry at the beauty and I cannot turn away for it is not separate from me... when love no longer plays our song it will echo... still it is not ours

and it seemed like forever that he had scanned the pages, Peering through the letters, trying to find the meaning under the words that he knew deep down were true... and the words became his new language he could use them and create sparkling sentences. But he knew that his understanding was like the glossy shimmering scatered over a deep ocean that he longed to bathe in... and one day without warning he looked up! And the rush of reality roared Pierced him deeply Ripped his heart out Beating still... And he sobbed in his pool of tears... Breathing in the beauty

and life was like the warm western winds as sea was kissed with setting sun flowing through her as her ... filling her emptying her... swooning into and through wonder itself no longer dependent on the swirling surface tension of iridescent hue, the utter amazement a constant explosion imploding simultaneously... it is always like the last bead the final brushstroke the last stitch the resolution of a series of notes or chords the moment when the sun kisses the sea or the lips an unending sigh the perfection of super completeness... indescribable unutterable supreme spaciousness appearing to separate and simultaneously kissing falling swooning disappearing into itself

There is a timeless blur when you are vaulted out of charted seas, Where you find your own wind that has the scent you longed for that you tasted in your dreams. and you can no longer tell if it is the winds blowing you or you are the wind and your steps leave no print on the ocean of tears flowing glowing in the moon light that pours through your tender nakedness... and the little girls laughed and danced as they held out plastic bags to catch the wind as they remembered flying. Kissing moon dreams in the vastness

and traipsing across this seamless sky words can never cut the vastness into pieces. they may whoop and swirl and sail in sunset dreamland, yet the wake of the ship never actually cuts the ocean in two. and your tears are never separate from the salty seas of love, and all your hearts desires are fulfilled when there is no longer trying. there is no separate control- ler of life with an on-and-off switch and a special knob tuning in the station you long to hear

and last night's rain sprinkled like tears on the window crystalline drops catching the morning sun reflecting on the canyon walls golden drops smiling effortlessly. deep silence of dawn and never any here or there or before or after in the stillness that sings so brilliantly

and tearbrushed painted dreamscapes like footprints in the sky never forming nor dis- solving never done nor undone. cloud dreams of castles dissolving and flowing into and through themselves with no place to land nor safe harbor to steer to. yet the sails back lit like lanterns with the orangy reds of sunset... there you are a flowing poem

he whispered the words of the sages and felt his hands lift off the handlebars and won- dered where he could find his wings to fly... but oh! his heart had to break a thousand times and his love had to bleed out into the dream... his tears had to explode and implode over everything and idea and dissolve the imaginary lines between inside and out between this and that... and crystalline emptiness overflowed as he realized it was never a magic a love a life that could be held or that was his to hold or that there was anyone to hold it... and the knowing feeling of seamless edgeless transparent beingness without edge or split or division anywhere filled him emptied him soared through him as him without end or beginning or any place to land wingless skinless he soared in an empty sky

Thought continues to weave the dream to try to unravel the mystery of this stunning magnificence. Yet it is all like glistening shadows dancing on an imaginary sea where lov- ers meet and sing... no longer looking to kiss the kiss of midnight with your unspeakable brilliance you are like a shooting star alive with your own vastness describing an arc in the vault of sky through which you vanish just as magnificently as you seemed to appear ... with one breath simultaneously in and out... the whoosh falling though the whoosh... always the first and last kiss

And her pajamas had butterflies on them but they did not give her wings. Try as she might she could never smell the flowers in the wallpaper. It was only a picture in a magazine she had folded and opened and folded so many times of the sun setting over the western oceans that the lines began to break up sea and sky into separate pieces. The last time she got the picture out she started to sob where was the beauty that she had longed for? And the lines dissolved in tears salty sweetness returning to the home she had never left... A shimmering song singing to itself gathering up the staves the notes fly off the lines and hum a primordial song of awe. Beauty sings through our empty hearts and paves the sunsets path with sparkly pebbles

Knowing we are life's objectified longing, the urge to sing of this, knowing it can never be kissed with words paints my dancing echo with colored sky like iridescence. It keeps my story alive. Always a thirst that quenches itself drinking deeply the poems that soar through me as they tumble down the canyon and swirl in reflecting whirlpools where I catch my reflection in your beautiful beautiful eyes

and where was her shadow in the rain or in the hush of darkness and when was her song separate from all songs and when were her tears separate from wetness everywhere and where was her breath separate from winds soaring and when were her footsteps separate from the dance of sorrow and joy of all and how could love be owned where did her heart end and the world begin? she was the rain and the wetness and the breath steaming tears streaming she was the faces she saw smiling weeping laughing singing how could she have ever believed she was one face one heart one breath one song among many

it was a constant knife blade piercing her chest to believe it was her love her life to hold a hole that could never be patched it had to explode and implode into everywhere and nowhere... and she peered into the flower to uncover to reveal its obvious beauty and majesty... why did it move her so? what was under the color the form the scent the softness the light the ache to know became the ache of this love and sorrow and joy and life itself could not be captured

Twisting and turning in edgeless freedom she lost sight of the ground and found herself pirouetting into endless sky. Vast beyond imagination, more spacious than she could have ever believed, more intimate than her very breath, closer than close in its infinite embrace, falling into and through herself she became all selves every face she saw was her own, every breath was her breath. the breath of life breathing through her the universe touching itself through her. raw skinlesss precious being this unowned life utterly sublime. This hyper awareness of being aware. of death, of wonder, this super vibrancy includes all the senses every pore of her being is saturated as awe. She was the magic the mystery of life looking at itself

empty shadows dance and sing in the tall moonlit forest. their song is but an echo you heard in last nights dream. their steps describe an empty space where someone used to live. they cannot be captured yet they are felt as a wind against your cheek, cradled in your own embrace, a self referential web of nothingness creating phantoms of desire... like a thousand folds of emptiness have created this day time dream... an origami swan sails on the sea of utter bereavement... all is lost nothing is gained... and the beauty of transparent sails transforms the edgelessness into something unbearably beautiful

golden afternoon sun kisses the canyon walls illuminating places that were hidden all day... clouds gather aimlessly in the north, a bird song echoes from wall to wall, measureless beautiful dreamlike source-less and uncatchable waves of joy burst forth in tears of awe... I move my hand and the canyon the wind the space the river our breath our feet dance as one flow. Timeless... And seeing that as wondrous is in itself wondrous

It's like I can hear the echoes of millions in every word uttered... every thought sings the chorus of infinity... reverberations of all selves spinning their tales from the same words soaring effortlessly skinless without purpose a constant union... I fly as the wind and the wind flies through me. I am unfindable yet I find myself everywhere I turn...

As birds swoop and swirl delighting in the taste of sparkles... Our lives a river of unnamed countless tears... The flowing Is us

your imaginary grip on the tiller and the stars dissolved into your own unimaginable beauty...and flowers bloomed showering yellow into the sun and you see your own reflection reverberating endless echoes of sky, and never really wonder where you have gone

and the afternoon rain slides off the edge of my umbrella, jewels reflecting my glistening tears, water of sky and sea kissing spinning tales of sea-dreams, and how I longed to remove my clothes and bathe in delight... colored raiment dancing footless songs, now the dance of timeless dreams... and waves swirl rainbows in puddles, fluid pictures dissolving as infinite color. My tears become the dance, lost in wonder of no longer wondering why the magnificence of knowing I was an unknowable song singing itself hearing itself touching tasting itself through me. I no longer cared to capture my shadow chase my tale, and suns slid through me as I disappeared into myself an infinitesimal membrane that separated me from you dissolved and I slipped inside you. I am a poem that writes itself. Fleeting description. Knowing I am a streaming water color thought dream Is unutterably wondrous

A shadow bird soars through the rippling waves. Bejeweled iridescent reflection dives into a sigh... the hush falls through Itself

Without the banks there is no river. Without direction there is no path. Without a path there is no tomorrow. Without tomorrow there is no now. Without now there is no you

echoes ripple across edgeless seas and crossing and flowing over and under and through the shimmering we can never really touch as we lose ourselves in each others beauty. Flowing in and through each other, Dancing in a moonlit reflection flying soaring this and that wings of love

and small inky black clouds sail in front of towering white ones then blend back into the storm... thunder echoes in the canyon and the birds are still ...stunned into silence the children stop their games... wind rushes down the canyon and water follows... and we run laughing with utter abandon into the rain

and you crept like a thief in the night and watched the moonlight play on breaking waves... gripped with terror and longing that your frozen heart might break open and you would drown in your own love... Tears flow rivulets pouring merging in rivers hunger for the shoreless sea

flowing over and through each other, Ripples reflecting above and below... And in between a shimmering Transparent jewel of wonder. No longer looking for a place to rest. No longer trying to grab handfulls of air to stop the fall. No longer trying to count the stars to fix your position, you fell into the falling and were Swallowed by your own love

and the morning which seemed drenched in shadow finally arrived and the dawn which had never been lost appeared like sparkling drops of frost thawing melting rivulets of wonder illuminating every feature with sun lit clarity, and how I lost my freedom when I believed I had it, there was no one left to be free or not free... the war was over and no one won or lost... all the rules slipped away and there was no one left to look for them... like tattered playbills my life lay scattered on the ground. Wind whipped up the pieces and they swirled into an illusion of cohesion but the wind dies down again and only the ripple of ancient songs sing a story of who I once was

It's like sitting on the edge of a cliff by the sea and you cannot make sense of the patternless patterns of the sea foam or clouds. Or the rhythmless rhythms of the waves. And you are transfixed by the unfathomable vastness the utter enormity of transparency. The weight of light streaming. And the unknowable indescribable sky like magnificence of not being able to grasp what is going on fills you empties you flows through you as you and inside and outside collapse into and through each other. you are lost in and as the supreme beauty of what you are. Infinite mirrored facets revealing countless shades and timbres of unimaginable beauty

Flowers bloom wilt fall leaves blow swirling so... Down the canyon's echoing walls where shadows danced effortlessly in moonlight dreams... trees slowly waltzing shadows meet here in a grove of love. In the end there is no one to understand or not Believe Or not And no one left to care

And what can be said about day without night or night without day... day without end or end without day... And where is the end or beginning to what spirals the thought dream. where in your wondering and wondering about who is what is what is this what is that what is what

So beautifully the dream of this and that paints and kisses and colors in a world without limits a world with lines a world with lines that are drawn in penciled in by a timeless eraser an origami whirl-o-graph folding in meringue and taste by placing lines between imagined things that are made up like you and me and spaces in between An imaginary inside an imaginary outside. Grasping reaching longing to consume itself in its own embrace. This dance of life for longing to embrace it self. Always embraced. Always the inside and the outside of the first and last kiss

LATE AUTUMN SONGS

Her utter nakedness astounded her... clothed in her own naturalness.
She could feel the warm summer breezes caress her cheek, the warmth of love caress her brow and no longer cared that it came from everywhere and nowhere.
Pattern less patterns danced across her brow and adorned her shimmering silhouette with color unending.... Realizing she was love's memories... a silent symphony of wonder singing her into being

Everything is nothing and not even that. Everything is empty, everything is full. Everything is a sigh a smile a tear an empty distant shadow dancing under a rose bush to a heartbeat a song heard by no one heard by everyone.

I am everything as I am nothing. An undefinable emptiness beyond empty neither moving nor non moving extending everywhere and nowhere indefinitely explodes and ricochets into infinite swirling pirouettes coloring unfindable lines with stories called time and you and me and a dance. A magnificent passion play painting itself with love and joy and sorrow and deep deep despair. The symphony is overwhelmingly stunning as I am the orchestra yet it plays itself resounding in the unknowable misty caverns of my brain.

Moon rises above the canyon walls and traces the delicate new growth on the trellis. It twists and twines in innumerable tendrils of shadow and shine and I cannot read the tales it tells, but I know the language of Spring. We all know intimately this dance of life, and some can know that they are, that we are, that this twostep is a fabrication. Most are bewitched by the lines but a very few have swallowed a magic potion of ultimate destruction and are drunk on love. Intoxicated with the dance knowing it is just that.

As the moon sails across the canyon bits and pieces of moon peer in between the branches of the pecan tree that reaches into sky. Yet never is the moon nor sky broken into parts. To seem to move and dance and shimmer on the pond requires imaginary pieces of here and there and someone to watch.

To be astounded at the beauty and power of words to paint in the parts, to fill in the space with a fullness so stunningly wondrous needs delicate tender eyes, your eyes my eyes our eyes of utter beauty.

All this wondrousness of a seemingly known world out of what can never be known or understood or captured as there is nothing outside of it, and no one to step outside of it and say 'oh yes, here is life! I am separate from it!'

There is no one who can escape this passion play as outside of the dance of you and me there is no one, or thing, not even nothing. There is no outside nor inside. There has never been a separate you nor others nor treetops dancing in the wind nor a someone or thing blowing and directing the wind the play the steps of your beautiful feet upon the path that has no end or beginning just a breath of song in the forest of vast spaciousness. As the trees grow and fall and waltz in the moonlight it's obvious that no one can manipulate or accept or reject or surrender to life as they are it. You are the wind and the tree tops dancing, the moon and the vault of sky. There is no wind nor trees nor sky nor darkness nor light nor moon nor beauty nor love to sail into your heart outside of this passion play we call life.

I reach out my hand and almost touch you as day kisses your heart through your beautiful eyes.

When all the questions burn themselves out there is a most delicious unknowing
a simple recognition that nothing can be understood or known or captured with words
ideas abstractions... as there are no things or non things
There is no one left to try to understand

there is utter peace in this life without trying
all effort comes to a complete halt.

....and nothing has any more or less meaning than the treetops dancing in the wind....

And you are the song as it sings itself. Reflecting reverberating ricocheting in infinite timbre and hue, Yet never separate from a song of thindering silence. A variegated syncopated rhythmless rhythm... where patternless patterns dance and swirl. A kaleidoscope of unparalleled beauty. A song of everything and nothing whips across the dreamscape and settles in your bones. And every secret pore of your being is ripped wide open unleashed with the singing of pure delight. A laugh in the distance. An echo of soundlessness. A sigh of a remembered kiss. A dream that fell through the horizon and was tangled in its own web of jewels

And you circled around an imaginary center and color and sound blossomed and receded like multi petaled flowers chasing themselves into a dawn where dusk resided. You are the water and the wetness, the liquid and the drinking, The emptiness and the fullness, The light and the reflection

Her sails unfurled at midnight as she became the moon and and its reflection Forever kissing on the sea of desire. No shore or harbor was needed Bathed in her own delight...

our tears flow down us like colored rain... showing us where our lines blend... watery dreams dancing into a mirage of skinless beauty... Soaring without shadows...or regret... a wake of nothing leaves no trace it falls into itself splashes reflect your beauty ...like a ripple on a still pond flows into and over and through it self without a trace... and wings form where sorrow slept

Springs flowing onto virgin ground... fresh newness everywhere. Delicate tracery of young ferns unfolding... and old ones brown beneath the earth breathing in sunlight and exhaling awe. Delighting in freedom that cannot be captured. A dance of memories that have not yet been dreamt or remembered. Songs flow in around and through you... and you can no longer find your part... the strings of your instrument... became untied and life strums you. And the wonder fills the emptiness its always a song you remember as it is sung. Falling from whose lips whose tears are running down your cheeks... They are un owned..... Your hand reaches out to dry anothers and you touch your own face crying. Its your hand... grasping the ropes of air that swing you in a lullaby, yet the lines float across the seamlessness and tickle words out of their hiding places. Reflected in teardrops dancing... shadows play along the walls and disappear into each other. A magnificent passion play where love blossoms and falls and the underlying sense of peace and ok-ness never ends..... and streaming through it all ....this sublime seamless ease ....perfumed with the most overwhelming sense of awe. drunk on love dancing in heaven's kiss

stars spiral outward and leave nothing behind... only a traceless path leading into your own heart and your part has always been perfectly played a sublime kiss constant union... it was simply an excruciating misconception that you were one half of a kiss

you no longer have to look at your feet to know how to dance the dance has always done itself. That desperate clenching trying to grasp the air there is no one to hold the pen and nothing to grasp

an empty dress... made of shimmering shadows... rainbow's tears sighing stream-ing through you as you ...memories of every story that has filled your heart.... endless beginingless timeless tapestries of infinite color and hue... overtones weeping though undertones caress inside and outside of empty faceted centerless jewels reflecting echoes of dawn of sunset of night of day... shine and shadow merge twist and twine and sing of beauty that cannot be uttered... the wonder of simply existing shines through you as a hyper awareness of awareness predominates we are all stories that have ever been or will ever be... unowned unsigned unabashedly unfettered and realer than real. vibrant beyond measure. an unowned life

And broken dreams like shattered glass gathered in between the cobblestones Illuminating her footsteps with constellations of love remembered. Kisses in the dark

and I wanted to paint the sky...but my hand fell into blueness...and the colors ran with tears uncaptured and the spaces between the branches swallowed me and I danced in starlight and starlight danced in me

And in the weaving and unweaving of the dream, this bejeweled essence of color, of light of sound exploding imploding smelled like loves delight. and the warmth of her own embrace flooded her smile with the knowing that all she saw and all whom she met were her own shining essence. Amorphous unknowable dreamlike, yet vibrantly alive. a kiss unrivaled. A diaphanous light garment revealing emptiness Dancing

And she watched her hands move methodically through the air no longer searching for abnormalities or gems, They wove a cats cradle not intending to catch anything. There were no things. Simply arabesques of rainbow hue dissolving into light... Bathing in the warmth and beauty of her own essential emptiness. Hollowed out in between the lines... Pouring love

It is neither joy nor sorrow. It is a bittersweet glow that sweeps you into the folds of itself and laughs and weeps with abandon. And you are it and it is you in the ever unfolding ever quivering tenuous tip that seems to divide what has never been and what will never be. A sublime aloneness that can never be touched nor kissed with words

in the unknown deep silence lying in the very heart of unfathomable depths where love's blood lays at your doorstep and whispers are born there is a dawning... and crystal blue waters flow iridescent in moonlight's gaze... falling into the depths of despair you become it reaching the heights of sublime joy you are not separate from it and soon the quickening in your chest the heartbreak that broke you... fills you and reflections of moonbeams dance across the surface of my tea... and I stir the starlight in and the miracle continues... I dissolve into the dream and laughter is heard echoing in the stars. And I reached in the moon and found the key to the universe as it unlocked all ideas of someone to be free... and empty sky spirals upwards and rainbows form and slide down washing every pore of my being with love

and the timeless empty streets of mind are flooded with ancient daydreams and words thoughts songs are shared creating a picture of reality and the wind propels me down the rain drenched streets and streetlights illuminate golden diamonds flooding... slipping into edgelessness my world is unbound... unwound by this knowing of not knowingness and though words can never capture my joy and awe I sing like a mountain stream dappled with starlight... the ink disappeared as it kissed the river... and even the ripples forgot about the ocean. And the winds rush around the streets of the village and no one asks where they come from or where they will go watching amazed at the swirling chip bags dancing with forgotten flowers faded. Like a rainbow bursting into bloom. Like your feet know where to step even on a rocky path

and I longed for Filigreed kisses appearing as fantastic love songs where I would always be held and never lost. Yet at the edge of the precipice it was like I was underwater and the lights sparkling on the surface reflected their rainbows on the sandy bottom and I could no longer tell which way was up... never lost never found when there's no longer anywhere to go

And the palm fronds dance... their tips pointing the way to endless sky. who knows where the bird has flown... her wings have let no trace except a melody you cannot quite remember. I have no order. the winds undone tie knots in the daydream and cannot find itself without a song to lay in. The borders are blasted dissolved in tears..... Yet there is no one to cry anymore without an outline of a tear. And a cheek to caress and a heart to touch. The very confines that you felt restrained you Blossom into countless petals touching hello goodbye hello

the idea of 'happiness' or 'love' was beginning to seem like a dream that would never ever come and yet my desire for love pierced me deeply and ripped me shredded me and emptied my dreams of love and magic and time until there was nothing left not even a skeletons dance

awakening is not a walk in the park. ya keep looking and looking for what can never ever be found a better moment... another moment... and all your dreams of what life or love should be start to crumble it just keeps smacking you in the face... over and over and over again that this is it whatever it looks like and you have no control over thoughts feelings sensations... of life itself you realize that all perception no matter what it looks or feels like happens all by itself... and that all perception arises equally and evenly without doing a thing... simply 'out of the blue' thoughts sensations feelings arise and spontaneously without any effort there is a recognition of them and it dawns slowly or hits ya hard that you have never been separate from what's going on. and in the end there is not even nothing left you are utterly empty... and there is not even a you to be empty

And a sigh of love rushed in. Caressed me found me animating my empty shadow dancing in the dark in the wake of loves demise

Right now, Just as you are. You are the gem of the universe. Eons of evolution have created an objectifying human brain that allows awareness to be aware of being aware through this magnificent streaming dream of separation. This dream of you that paints and erases itself simultaneously. Only through you is there love. And beauty. And wonder

Right now. Just as you are. Your bum on the chair. Your eyes scanning these lines. Your fingers sliding across the screen. Your breath. Your heartbeat. Your longing to find an answer, or a key to an imaginary door... Searching for a better way. Longing for what you know not. This is the dream singing itself it happens all by itself. Looking and feeling like anything at all. Knowing you are the dream Will not stop it. This is it coyote

Creeping softly the dawn brushed his brow with a kiss of reflected moonlight. an untrodden path was illuminated with facets of broken dreams and he watched his feet dance as the path fell away his dreams of tomorrow cast out in the fallen night... dried leaves scattering golden dust in starlight's gaze

So beautiful this amorphous simultaneously self arising self erasing thought dream weaving and unweaving this passion play of you of me of we... Staves of birds flight paths colored in by clouds delicately softly like a butterfly kiss in mid air

He looked furtively behind him as he ran away from his shadow, and the shadow running wove the dream ...footsteps lost themselves on the path as light fell under his hat... frozen leaves on the sidewalk blow away and leave an imprint of an empty heart... and the winter winds ripped the last leaves off the trees spiraling falling swooning blazing in ecstatic wonder into the sky... And the canyon waltzed silently clothed in the yellowy oranges of sunset. Breathing the sigh of nighttime deeply

that Big beautiful enormous gaping hole in your heart. That overwhelming emptiness you feel. That longing to love so deeply you lose yourself. And that fear of losing all that love... That is the great ache that you are. Emptiness overflowing an unadorned rippling shimmering rainbow hued reflections a wakeless wake on stormy seas. Can't you hear it? It is your song, Singing you.

He tried to remove the blue from the sky, and as his hands moved through the vastness Unseen ripples cried out with the lack of love. Ravens never looked behind as they soared over the canyon walls, barren trees seemed to capture the sky with death Reaching...and star light scattered diamonds in his eyes

Running her fingers through her thought stream rippling dream waves weaving the dream, rainbow trout shimmered under the ice as sun filtered through crystalline snow gently brushing the Herons wings... losing his bearings as unutterable Beauty wept in sun falls....the enormity of stillness singing the dance of echoes dreaming blew wide open his ideas of now and forever and everything and nothing

time could not seduce him ideas of rest could not move his feet.... Yet words soared through him and colors formed swirling swooping on ropes of light, his fingers combed the vastness and melted wings of tears cascading as wonder thundering hooves a back-beat to his aching heart... vast untamable fathomless brilliance pierced him deeply and ushered in an unsigned beauty that wrote his name in the wind

Fractured rainbows fell into sentences that spoke of infinite color perfuming the marrow of song with bejeweled space dripping flowing through her as her.... an essence of star-light reflected a world so vast so unimaginably heart wrenching wondrous songs soared through her... watercolors painting erasing her story on the river. And I had no words as the sun crocheted a long tendril of emptiness around my song

So beautifully inescapable this thought dream of you of me of we, Weaving itself with tendrils of emptiness... space twining space with Ropes of light and Tattered dreams... Flowing singing sailing

For never existing but almost... Trying to grasp it or touch it is it weaving itself... Daydreams night dreams tumbling into the the crashing waves, Where there is not even a sigh, Or lovers breath to kiss them. It's a crochet dream unraveling as it simultaneously weaves itself. Shadows shimmering in the sunset dawn, love writes itself with radiant shadows dipped in rainbows. And what of love he asked What of rainbows kissing? Where was the Dawn when he remembered it? What became of his shadow he had lost one wintry morn? Where were the dreams of futures remembered? And where were his hopes of the brilliance of loves desire? Where were his questions that had played him like shooting stars animating his heart... He lost himself in his reflection and no longer cared to find it. Dipped in beauty Shadows sing Of light of wonder of the utter ease of shining... And cicadas rush in the brushes and sparkle in their own delight... And where were his tears Of love remembered? Lying in the cool summer grasses moon glow in his eyes as his lover sang him songs that cooled his weeping. He could not find them, as he had slipped into his own love. And sublime aloneness wrote his song With an ache that sang ever more. He was the wake of loves demise. Not one iota of hope for other remained. Yet he did remain as simply a song in his own heart.

the crown topples off
the anchor is lost
drifting rudderless in uncharted edgeless seas...
Here it is love's heart essence that fills your sails
as it empties them...
playing tunes that have never been heard or lost
spreading
everywhere

in and through you as you
the dancing itself
was never found
yet felt deeply

they sang alone
together
dissolved into themselves

Every breath was lost every tear had been shed every song had been sung. The mad dance of love was over. There was not even nothing left. Yet life flowed through him like empty waters and began to tap Tap Tap Ebb and rush on the shoreless ocean. Where no harbor could be found. Silent eddies danced and swirled into a memory and dreams of love remembered lit the rippling overtones Into a song of joy. Yet winds blow and have no hold on sky. Tears dry. And lovers weep. And life continues. Madly laughing Forever drowned In your own tears...

Silent arpeggiod fan taled dreams
Echoing in sky between here and there
No hand blows the wind
No one sings... Naked skinless homeless awe

And a shadow bird flies over the rippling waters... The shimmering holds an empty footprint. Leaves decked as golden lanterns swirl from the trees and sing dusk into the canyon. Always only this, He said And smiled an empty smile that sang of loves demise... Battles lost Blood spilt Screams echoed Moonlight danced... Enough he said... This is enough... And he was the sigh, The shadow and the empty footprints, And Dawn brought a dew That skimmed the surface of the sea of dreams. The ground had collapsed. All and everything fell into and through itself, and Blue butterflies gathered on the edge of nothing

It was his own love It had always been. There had never been another. These were his own tears. Yet not his. He had never left home, yet his heart was an empty shadow Gathering moonbeams by the side of the road Looking for passersby to fall in love with.... His heart an open book For all and everyone to see... For without love He could not find himself, There was simply nothing left..... Just the wind ..... Soaring Laughing weeping singing songs of wonder and light... far up the canyon there was no one to sing to... further up the canyon there was no one to sing... Here yet not here... There yet not there. The shadow bird sings

and the desire to escape tethered the moon to a rosebush in the back yard. he saw it every night and tried to loosen the light plucking thorns out with his tongue as the petals sang of softness unbridled and color drank him a drought like no other the tankard spilled the sides fell away as the bottom dropped out..the moon loosed itself and he found himself lost. Suspended as nothingness light reflections longed to touch again... and it was love that brought his shadow back moon light shimmering

sun kiss'd tender beauty.... wet delicate I's touching in reflected mirrored touch multicolored brilliant hues merging blending never separate never together... tattered remnants of love's glow fade and bloom in an ungraspable immediacy... fringed tears fray and weave themselves into infinitely petaled tapestries.... memories of smiles and laugher echo in the winds of loves demise never ending never beginning always ending always beginning

you have been to the edge and seen there is not even nothing outside the dream... and realized you are the dream... and you return... clothed in wonder... And life continues Madly laughing Forever drowned In your own tears... Soaring naked skinless all your pockets your heart your innermost being has been ripped inside out. There is nothing left to hide and no where to hide it. Every pore of your being is vibrantly alive Singing... And you are the sigh, The shadow, and the empty footprints... And Dawn brings a sparkling dew That skims the surface of the sea of dreams..... sun kisses shadows dancing... and it's only the tears drying on the pavement that reveals our essence

words fly in as and through the emtptiness.... and cannot catch the overwhelming unknown... no longer needing to trap a moment....songs sing themselves and we meet here in utter wonder. And always living in the middle... a space between a breath... and your lips... this trembling tenuous grasp less ness... fills you more than any wish fulfilled

Names.... like arrows melting in the sun, and yet always undone ...nothing can be made out of winds... songs sing themselves and can never pinpoint our hearts... like breadcrumbs ...eaten as they fall... forgetting a path to nowhere... as the flowing we cannot tell where one tale begins and another ends... a kiss of nothing...like butterfly wings ....paint shadows in ripple's memories... yet felt oh so deeply.....this undeniable aliveness simply blows you away... the cage of words has become transparent .. it is freedom beyond any idea of being free or bound

painted on a curtain of diaphanous moonbeams ... starlight gleams and sees its beauty only by its reflection... the sails burned as the boat drifted .... never on it's moorings never had a wheel... like a mirage floating in a dream.... there was never any thing at all... it is utterly bewildering when you can't find up or down... when you scramble for the edges of the fast moving river and find only water and you look for a sunrise and discover the darkness has ended when sun and moon kiss and the seas pour into the sky and all words erase themselves ...as your fiery ship sinks ablaze with wonder...... eyes wide open..... you spread your wings into the vastness... soaring un-encumbered by feathers

she gathered the dishes after the feast and wandered in the kitchen... tattered dishcloths like old wigs hung by the sink... she watched a lifetime of resentment and longing go down the drain there was no need to fill her empty bowl... as it was no longer hers.. that ache in her heart had filled the world... and the lines between the old and the morrow could no longer be found... joy and sorrow had merged and there was no concern to capture life the heart of the matter... the trembling pulsating between this and that were seen to be timbre and hue of song itself... and it continued without a singer... only empty reflections echoing across the rocky cliffs where winds rode the shadows... and ravens vied for the symphonic caverns... wet impermeable and deep neath misty ranges where clouds were left unhindered... a lifetime of imaginary barriers built... a scaffold of this and that... suddenly dropped away... and the winds and the sun and the shadowy moon continued to dance... without any dancer

Wind whispers through an imaginary membrane and forms my lips my breath my song Light streams through an imaginary magical prism. Painting infinite color and hue and my eyes to see them

Timpani ablaze in this edgeless night. Drumming out the notes and melody and music chords and that without a breath, without a pause, not even nothing can be heard. A dance a kiss a heartbeat Singing you and me and we into being. It cannot be captured nor understood or explained or believed and yet it is obviously always so. Oneness swallows Twoness swallows oneness

This is it coyote. this is your one and only fleeting momentary, and it is not even yours. You cannot catch life you are it. Life passionately kissing itself deeply through your lips your eyes your ears your fingers your beautiful delicate touch... and the story writes itself weaving every thing into itself. A constant changing multicolored translucent light gown swirling around an empty center

and tendrils of emptiness untied the secrets that were locked inside the storm... and loosened her hair from its lofty castle... winds rushed through the vacant house... where dreams once lived... and hopes flourished... where memories gathered on lonely shelves... awaiting discovery... of loves lost and found... and children looking into a future knots untied themselves... and she found herself ...just as she had always been... utterly naked... clothed in wonder... a hush... before the dance light... before the rainbow the breath.. before the song yet needing two lips... for this ...the one and only kiss

most people have an ah ha moment when they see something or hear something or feel something so intense or beautiful there are no words... the mind is silent.. for a moment... and thought comes back and describes it.. there was a feeling that you were not there...

or that you were part of or blended with the sunrise or symphony or the wind caressing your face dancing in the tree tops. So they try to get that utter stillness back.. that peace that was so overwhelmingly wondrous they might look for others who proclaim a path or method to regain that sublime peace. and no matter what the person does or tries not to do... there might be glimpses... but they do not last as all efforting, all looking, all non efforting simply confirm the belief in other in more in next, in the mother of all beliefs, in separation

trying to quiet the mind is a trick many use meditation and as it seems to work... when it does not give the permanent effect you desire you just blame yourself and try harder creating an never ending loop of more and more seeking which substantiates the belief in a looker a seeker and something to get. this sublime quiescence of which we sing is the recognition of unicity and it cannot and need not be contrived or achieved or attained anew as it is always on merely felt or not. so looking for a center a peace a stillness creates and substantiates the illusion of a solid and fixed and stable you and there is nothing solid nor stable nor fixed.

there is simply nothing the imaginary character can or cannot do to get this you will never get this it is a profound shift in perception in which the sublime brilliant shoreless ocean of the knowing feeling of seamlessness is always on that occurs in the brain. there is no center that you can arrive at ...you are like a centerless jewel... shimmering iridescence swirling around an empty center... you are an imaginary reference point around which all other imaginary 'things' and 'moments' revolve

Sparkling iridescence slips out of your imaginary grasp and pours through your fingers. You never could catch a moment and save it for later. Yet the raindrops splashing on the river make gorgeous ripples, Lost as they fall, Not this not that not here nor there, Slipping in between the lines. Not everything nor nothing...

echoes of raindrops trail down the window water merging into water rivulets coalesce and separate colors sliding into and off the wetness hiding and revealing formless seamless images this sublime edgeless hush ripples dancing shadows in puddles of streetlight

clouds streaming over and through clouds weaving magic tapestries basking in jeweled starlight gaze. water drowning in itself, sadness pouring into sadness, rivers of tears pouring into oceans. the bittersweet saltiness of unowned vastness. you emerge naked and raw seeing like never before this seamless timeless original beauty unadorned with nets of words. Yet magically strung like lights in the darkness this ever emerging newness of all and everything, you are this magic it brushes your cheek with your own softness and its touch leaves no imprint as the words slide into the vastness and you dissolve again into the slipstream

Lost unclaimed photographs tattered by winds swirled into forgotten pictures of who you once were. A life unowned waltzed down the canyon dancing in the tree tops. Inside exploded into outside into vast unnamable edglessness and love and light streamed everywhere and nowhere through you As you. Untouched untrammeled uncontained unkissed, as your lips become the song. Falling through the lines you lost your footing as you slipped into the sky and vast sky like spacious wonder clothed you as you stepped naked into the dream

what it is that has no name nor non name yet is utterly obvious what is it that cannot be captured or held yet holds you caresses you from the inside out what is it that cannot be known or touched or kissed yet lies between the touching and the touched the kissing and the kiss the breath and the song how can this overwhelmingly felt sense of pure unfettered wildly naked spaciousness sublimely present the taste of taste

whispering gently always this is it. there is no other. it is you who kisses who holds and who is being kissed and embraced, the light and the reflection, you are this poem of streaming unutterable beauty reflecting resounding echoing madly without time nor place in every thought and feeling and touch wonder adoring itself life kissing itself delight delighting in itself mega tears mega hearts. Unbearably beautiful

EARLY WINTER SONGS

Oh I know what it's like to reach a point of complete and total despair
I know what it's like to feel like you will never ever get this
And I know what it's like to feel like you are getting it like you are getting somewhere and
have that rug pulled out right underneath you

And I know what it's like to pretend that I no longer want this when deep down it is all I
had ever wanted

Not knowing what it was but desiring it greatly
Overwhelmingly so
so that I spent all my days and nights trying to get something
I did not even know what it was

And to discover finally that what I had been seeking had been here all along

Simply nakedly obviously so

What I had always been awareness aware of being aware
Through the beautiful magnificent transparent lens of self

It cannot be achieved it cannot be attained it is not separate from you it is life touching
tasting feeling it's own aliveness through you

Life happening utterly spontaneously all by itself
Without any effort without anything needing to be done

A veritable feast
And uninterrupted indivisible symphony of what we call perception
And the simultaneous inseparable recognition of it
Just like that
Just like this
Marvelous and superb

And everything is included where else could it possibly be
Thoughts of past thoughts of future the whole range of human emotion and experience
all of it a gem a jewel
Spinning wildly
swirling twirling whirling
creating an imaginary center

There never was any other better more or next
Or anyone to get this
or anyone to arrive
or anyone to get there
There is no here nor there

A taste of sweetness was never stolen or bought. Always on the tip of your tongue yet it cannot sing ...infinite strands of stillness dance in waves crashing on shoreless seas and where was the shimmering she lost in her pocket of unsung songs

Inside out and outside in, in between the in between, kisses kissed themselves in wall less canyons, sourceless reflections fell through their own mirrored kisses as your hand fell through the vastness as you longed to catch a piece of sky. Day fell through night as your fingers dissolved... deep deep despair crashed into unbearable joy, dark lost in light, light in dark. And the dance sways in stillness as you sing in the silence of sound. Love reigns tears... and the words you so longed to hear merge inside and outside without sides leaving a shimmering transparent brilliant spaciousness

Space falls into space. Light into light. Fire burns fire. Oceans pour into oceans of vast unknowable quietude that sing unendingly of butterfly kisses roaring in your blood. like moon pouring reflections into the waters that you longed to drink from, you see only a beautiful clear light of your own love and emptiness

That undeniable hunger for an ineffable taste of the sweetness you feel in your belly and long to uncover you cannot mouth the words that kiss your heart so deeply so penetratingly perfect... This ache for what you know not, Yet you hear it always... On the tip of your tongue.....

Songs in the night Pierced by love's heart magic. Eviscerated by your own love. Speechless. Breathtakingly ravishingly beautiful ...this unsung note... Your very ungraspablilty the very essence of no essence perfumes the dream with seamless ease nothing is another concept. This is an emptiness beyond empty... So vast so excruciatingly devastatingly ravishingly beautiful that it has no name as it cannot be captured. It has no edge, It is not an it or non it. It has no essence, Yet it permeates all and everything with its obvious beauty... It has no qualities... Yet it is felt deeply... It has no words, Yet every word sings it. Beyond imagination yet realer than real, the moon shines with lovers light and weeps at its own radiant majesty

pure like untrammeled space, Infinite beyond measure. A silence so vast so all encompassing. The hum of a sigh burning windswept rocks strewn across the desert Singe your last heart strings, Ashes blown across the Rippling sands sparkle just so ...the death of emptiness

And she searched for words that would twist the handholds of hearts and minds into weeping shadows... for words that would blow your mind more than a hurricane, and heat your desire more than fire, And soak the edges of your smile More than tears

and how could you be separate from your tears? how could you be separate from touch or sight or sound or light? how could you be separate from breath? how could you be separate from your heartbeat? how could you be separate from emotion? from love? it is only because of words that it seems like there is a feeler a weeper.... a lover

what is in between the inside of the inside, what is outside of everything? where is nothing? where is nowhere? Where is where? when does a thought begin and end? when does a moment begin and end? when does a feeling begin and end? catch one put it in your pocket with your self. catch a river... cry a river and drown... Clouds spilling shadows across the desert.... moon loosens her clothes as they dance by...Shimmering baseless reflections light up flowing shadows dancing a pas de deux where feet are discovered only in the dance. In the kiss we find our imaginary lines just as we fall into and through each other... Lost in the vastness of our beautiful I's

when kisses lose their lips yet sing of loves ravishing beauty words seem to capture a taste of what has no essence or source and the sun weeps at your immeasurable beauty

And the love you long to feel so deeply, Yet fear, Knowing it will devour you... Plunges its tongue into the deepest darkest secret places you did not even know existed, And chews out your very marrow... rips your heart inside out your skin and lips and teeth and bones melt in this heat your smile taunts you as it dissolves your song sighs in this love ... and Dawn melts away the shards of midnight as morning mists evaporate in the clear light that licks your eyes of knowing clean... ravished by your own love, Yet knowing love was never yours. Nor life your hands your gut your heart lies empty. A shadow bleeds Yet walks among the living. Swooning into the lovers he sees. Caught by his own reflection In their I's

She tried to take the wetness out of her tears, But the saltiness was too sweet... She drink fully her own love, And the cup of emptiness dissolved on her tongue

when the costume is woven with moonglow... and there is nothing underneath... footless steps dance by themselves... and there is no need to reach an imaginary next...the sigh of the ever emerging ever blooming ever wilting immediacy sings most wondrously... how marvelous when it is no longer believed that the pirouettes are instigated by the dancer... or the pas de deux is planned... and how supreme this knowing that my face is fleeting echoed memories ... it feels like a love song singing itself

winds sweep dragon clouds over the sun... growling thunder announces the storm.... trees dance and their fullness is revealed... all effortlessly happening...the clouds rain then they pass... leaving no trace... desert storm... such magnificence!

Rushing flowing streaming flying Slippery sliding down the rainbow of delight, I sip the nectar of absolute endlessness .. and with absolutely no place to land I catapult into the vastness of the brilliant radiant vault of pure space... and when all boundaries are dissolved there are no more empty spaces that need to be filled, and no longer cloaked contained hidden in our prison of beliefs, we are left raw and naked and the light floods in. It pierces our very being with awe and wonder and amazement and a delicious knowingness that this brilliant timeless flow is a miracle what ever it looks or feels like.

And the leaves and the wind are one dance... effortlessly naturally simply so.... without reason or rhyme.... and completely without any compulsion to discover any meaning I dance as the leaves in the treetops and everywhere I look there is only this dance and I cannot conceive of there being separate things that are somehow reacting to each other like billiard balls.... or that there is a plan.... or a source..... or a script or a place where it needs to arrive and I sing of this unicity and I watch as others listen and put my song into boxes of already conceived ideas of what this is like....and the wind continues to dance and swirl and blow through the canyon

slipping silently through her shadow... heartbeat at midnight... the glow of moon shinning through her as her... unadorned ,,,skinless... awe shimmering like butterfly kisses...

she danced through the dream unafraid of nowhere... tipsy from the kiss of emptiness the fullness ran through her veins... like water like wine like an aging sorrow singing the evening star to sleep. As midnight walks with baited breath, the moon sings love songs over the sea. The utter hush before dawn swirls into your brain and never leaves. An unrelenting taste Of midnight sun. Love and you were never separate. Arising inseparably as the moon sighed its empty breath, the the tree top's silhouette began to dance and colored in the dream of darkness. love is like a wave that flows across a forgotten tear

She tried to smooth the air with her breath ...the mist enveloped her as the sun pierced the last remaining clouds. Adrift rudderless on a sea of dreams. Orb of fire slides across the vault of blue and longs to kiss its reflection. There is no clear without cloudy. No two without one, and no thing or non thing that can be measured. The increments of movement are dream points... where does day slide into night and what happened to the line between inside and out?

You reach for a tear you might have shed long ago...like a shadow of a dream you no longer remember but the tears have rippled into a vast unrelenting ocean. yet the reflections are so beautiful...the colors so enticing your hand falls through the glassy mirror and you drown

We are our stories as they weave and unwind their colored jewels into an unsung tapestry that pulses and shimmers and trembles in the light, where passion fills and empties a dusty street that holds empty footsteps that danced... Once Vibrantly with belief in the story. Now Gone

There is a bittersweet river where love plunged her heart and drifted away as she merged into the current of feeling and sensation. The utter weight of light flowing into its own lightness. The clear pure marvel of awe pours into and lights up wonder itself. As we are the river and the wetness and the knowing of it. The ease that we longed for that was always here Simply went unnoticed. Ahhhhhhh ......sings the river, Welcome home, I love you, I am you. It is sad and bittersweet and poignant how life Brushes your heart Onto the page. That has no edges, Or center. A watercolor Bleeds Into the dream. As overflowing colors flood and fade, A dream of unknowing.... Warp and weave A fabric Of you And me... And misty distant trails that no one will climb... an ever blooming flower this ever emerging unfolding undoing what was never done ... Oh how wondrous the colors sing flowing without edge or center.. She thought she heard a face in the moonlight, Tracing tears down the sidewalk as memory lost its grip. Writing the word river on the river cannot capture the flowing or the wetness or your reflection as you peer into it

Constantly watching imaginary lines form around an empty center,,,colors forms sounds textures varied of hue and timbre ... as soon as one foot starts to move the entire dance sings itself ...falling into and through itself without direction or place... A living dream

And she rain naked clothed in colored rain and leaned back her head laughing ..like this... Every step like a seed dancing the day into life. Footfalls not quite hitting the ground ... never a mark or trail... Gossamer light wings shimmered in delight at the sight of the storm the calm could not be trampled ...nor the light darkened ... yet her essence was memories ...even love had lost the war that no one won

time dies... into the hush... the pause... the silence that is always on... sparkling in the depths... under the storm ...or calm above... the momentum of a lifetime ...dissolves a crystalline sea without harbor...and no need to find one untouchable... uncreated... it need not and cannot be contrived or maintained

And words lines like filigreed percussions of emptiness swirling reverberating... echoes fill your heart resounding nothingness dissolving in emptiness... full yet empty... nothing to be found... snail creeps on the sidewalk, he may be crushed. Yet only we know of death. Only we know of life. Only humans know of this amazement that blows us away... light melting into light it puddles on the sidewalks and leaks into your being... there is no barrier between you and your tears it was only a thought that seemed to obscure the brightness... it was only a memory that seemed to create a path back to itself. The chorus of your own love song has never been hidden. it penetrates your dreams night and day it can never be forgotten, for it is everything and nothing continually appearing and resolving ...falling into itself

Tossing her shoes into the river she watches the emptiness engulf the night... Waves uncurl lost in backwards reflections... Moon sails unencumbered, Without care if another glimpses his lovelight

There really is no thing you can capture and call sadness... Can you step outside your emotions? Thought swirls...and in the words all things are born. Who has emotions/ You are them. Nothing is separate from what's going on is there? you say you feel separate well... that is part of what's going on. Do you feel separate from the feeling of being separate? Imaginary separation is created by thought.

Pigeon bathing in puddles... Walking typing crying... Rich and full beyond measure this thing we call life...and her fingers bled as she strummed through the scripts... and her heart fell through her life... an open book naked, unowned, the pages flew across the meadow ... so beautiful ... like white pigeons love letters flung into the sea... shining shimmering rippling songs for no one

no longer trying to trace her path... the ground fell away ...her footfalls could no longer be found as the edges crumbled into dust.... washed away in tears all that was left was the most precious jewel ... yet centerless... shimmering... falling in love with everything and nothing as she slid down the drain into what is

and when it hits ya ... it hits hard like dawn sweeps the canyon it is unstoppable this is really and truly all there is and all your dreams of how it should be could be simply vanish and you cannot remember why you wanted to paint a rainbow on the sky but, Oh! you remember the anguish of trying...What were we doing grabbing handfuls of air...trying to pinpoint a star... Trying to swallow sky

Painted with rainbows dipped in tears she slid into emptiness as the world blew by on a dream. And shadows dance and play shifting across the sidewalk. And it is known that it is a dance... utterly beautiful these thoughts these stories woven of gossamer wings... transparent iridescence leaving traceless shimmers in their wake.... and her dance moved the stars and the mountains and the sun cried knowing its fleeting beauty

Kissing themselves the lips disappear and only the essence of love remains ...The vessel of longing spills into itself, and tears illuminate the universe with a punctuating joy... Swallowed by your own untouchable magnificence.... Inseparable like the sun's rays

Looking for a place to touch down to rest to get off that roller coaster of hope and fear... Shadow dancing... We longed to escape our very existence... We remember screams of the battle... the bloody ground ...the excruciating pain of dying, and we sit by the campfire in the meadow... dead bodies buried all around and tell our stories and we watch some sparks fly in the night and return to the fire as others simply fly into starlight

and sometimes when you're surfing you can reach out and touch the side of the wave... fingers dipped in swirl and sometimes when you least expect it the sun shines right through you and sometimes when the package you tried to stuff your afflictions in comes undone... the wave swallows you and sometimes... as if by magic... the magic unties you and sometimes... your reaching fingers...touch an arabesque quite marvelous... is no longer separate from the moon and the hush of midnight is your very breath... and the roar of canyon winds... sings your name... as it sails through your hair your skin your teeth your blood your bones...and you are the wind and the wind is you and you realize it has always been this way

your very heart your very love explodes into the night...and your heartbeat is everywhere... this and that... magnificently unfolding... weaving and unweaving the dream the dance the song ....with jewels of tears like rain like sorrow like joy like nothing at all... an empty breath subsides into the sand glistening in the sunset on the edge of a shoreless ocean ...where even love cannot find a harbor all anchors have been ruptured like the sails of her dreams... tattered flying magnificently in uncharted seas... We just knew it was magic didn't we trying to slide down a rainbow we slid up the other side as we were catapulted into vastness

An ever blooming flower always at the peak of perfection. An unfindable spacious momentary between the blooming and the wilting. When time dies life becomes immeasurably wondrous. Far beyond anything we coulda ever ever ever wished for or imagined. As the dance continues, as we arise in the twostep

We are memories swirling ... dreams written with disappearing ink ...colored tears on the river ....hearts bleeding into a past that never was coagulating into a future that will never be. We are wonder inseparable from the wondrousness... Immeasurable, vast Beyond comprehension, and yet there is nothing here...Utterly empty. A desert bleeding into the sun... Spilling leaking flooding pouring into and through itself. A Still pond at the hush of midnight Sings

memories inform the unfindable present. They wrap up the flowing into boxes. We are infinite Russian dolls ...packages of unfolding out folding jewels sparkling in the midnight sun. The presents fall apart as soon as the wrapping is seen. Ribbons of imaginary timelines falling merging into the flowing, Colored dreams are the river where tears fled as our dreams of future slid into a picture of what we once were

and every secret pocket where you used to hide ...turned itself inside out... and there was no place to put a moment and no one left who wanted to capture it. in the misty wet caverns of your mind there dwelt an image of a moonbeam that swept through you.. and left a memory of a footprint illuminated by a forgotten shadow... emptiness spirals and light seems to flow into light and Oh! the shimmering reflections so beautiful your utter nakedness weeps. You look down at your feet as the dancefloor fell away ...and starlight fell through you as you. Reflecting the vastness that you had always been... And yet ...how marvelous a kiss a hug ...Love, The dance of two. Sublimely Bittersweet this dream of separation. This magicians tale. This virtual world. This dream of you of me of we....

Imploding exploding into and through everywhere and nowhere, nothing and everything. Loving living dancing on the edge of a feather between love and nothing at all. You step lightly into the dream Clothed in rainbow tears. Bathed in wonder. As clear centerless light reflects through the lens of self and erupts in a plethora of rainbow hue and a riot of silent sound and calm fury creates this passion play we call life. and laughter and awe and profound peace are the baseline and love the richness of it all. Edgeless centerless seamless being. Not lost not found nor no concern with place or time. Softer than soft. Sweeter than sweet, The morning song... Love's ancient memories sing us into existence

Through this, In this, as this Primordial vastness we soar and there is no end nor beginning. Yet We die. And a sublime echo of profound peace stills our hearts. A hush that cannot be sung

and as shadows waltzing through the kaleidoscopic shifting shadow dance.... we meet in the touching and find for an instant our feet move together as we fall into and through each other and lose ourselves again. For we are truly floating soaring, not on air or through space, but as nothing... nor or less than whispers of memories.... the remembrance of a kiss moves a heart that used to be mine... we are but empty silhouettes made of rivers of tears and laughter... just your smile and my world explodes

and the falling is falling and there is no harbor no place to put an anchor or crown and the swirling falls through the swirling and you find your self beautifully lost and even the lostness looses itself... and you reach out your hand to taste the waters and are enchanted with the reflection of sky and sea and sun and you and the rocks and seaweed flowing through the vast unknowable ...and a hush overwhelms you and you fall through that... and that wow and that silence never leaves

walking endlessly across the desert dream.... feeling like you are lifting you heavy feet and your heavy heart... dying of thirst yet you cannot drink the sand... mirages reflect imaginary signs up ahead... the trackless path is even well trod... like a gully your feet in circles in circles... perhaps your tears will puddle in your empty footsteps and you will catch a glimpse of the sky laughing behind your reflection and you will turn and face the vastness you have avoided.... and the tsunami that has been just behind you will eat you alive and you will emerge an empty shadow...dancing alone... here's a twostep a waltz a lovers tryst the clear air shimmering just so... no longer do you long to drink the shadows after they have swallowed you...every bit and particle of sand so spectacularly illuminated...and yet the knowing feeling of seamlessness ...sublime beyond measure

And the cool desert moon shimmered on the whispering sands beguiling lost and lonely travelers in the desert dream. enchanting love songs beckoned from afar... what was their hearts desire? where was the key to their hearts they could not fathom. Ravenous yet with no mouth they could not drink the light. Yet they followed paths worn and forgotten. Foot falls in the hush

some noticed fellow travelers leave the campfires late at night, Transfixed on a shooting star. Some simply remained by the campfires where there was much talking and arguing about what the water would feel like

only a very few realize that they have been traveling in circles. Creating a dream of outside and inside. For them The wandering stopped. There was no where left to go. And no urge to find what did not exist. They were not lost nor found, yet starlight streamed through their empty shadows...Rippling across the waters of home

the dancefloor collapsed and the morning sun crashed through an evening star we simply cannot see ourselves without each other...when it is known and felt that there is truly nothing there... everywhere you look you see your own tears your own beauty unowned flowing magic life ...love flows through you as you a shimmer a whispering dance echoes singing in starlight streaming flowing merging falling into and through a glance a song of moonlight at dawn... a wistful song streaming echoes in the dark where lovers meet in utter nakedness... Knowing she existed only as this enchanting dream this virtual reality of clouds catching the first rays of sun as it slides above the horizon... this pseudo reality of birds singing as they awaken to a new day... this magicians tale of friends lovers meeting by the sea .this hologram of kisses... this story of ancient dreams whispering love songs in the roaring waves...this passion play of conflict and resolution... The wars continue. Yet the deep untouchable sublime peace of a bottomless shoreless ocean remains, And is always perfumed with a most wondrous sense of awe

As life simply does itself. Desire the movement... Of mountain springs gathering into streams dancing laughing down canyons singing across rippling meadows rushing roaring longing for the sea

Life and light flow through me like winds with primordial wings glistening alighting on their own iridescence. Like light soaring through the colored fullness of vast uncontained immeasurable space... the weight of light itself pouring flowing rushing roaring tasting its own delight as they spill through this crystalline magnificent dream that I am

I love how thoughts paint my magic and it slides away as soon as it is tasted ..light spills through the morning and sings through my kiss.... and wonder floods the world and caresses my song with filigreed crystals that catch the light in iridescent rainbow delight... tears streaming from the sky paint trees and rocks with dark streaming shadows... and opalescent clouds flow and merge into dragons ever meeting ever parting.... how an ache for yesterday's day dreams used to paint the morrow with borrowed kisses.... and now an ever emerging kiss, As life tastes it's own mystery through me

Shallow falls through deepness and light through darkness. Here slid through there, mundane slides into sublime as all and everything sparkles in its own reflection Rich lush beyond measure.... Soaring skinless bathed in sky ...Trapeze artists paint the sky... Imaginary ropes of space that tethered past and future into a knot called you blew away in the hush that sang your name. Walking a tight rope of hope and fear to an ever looming end lost its grip as the knots untied themselves to reveal... Nothing.... time collapsed into itself and ricocheted into waterfalls of wonder. Suns slide across the vault of sky every breath your first and last

Threads of emptiness filled light shadowed memories and untied tendrils of tender beauty .....unweaving dreams of the morrow. Tasseled moonbeams softly brushed your wet cheeks. Where did these ancient tears arise? How could I not have recognized their beauty?

Melting softly into the slip stream of life ...... Quenching your unending thirst is this unending drought of life drinking itself through your lips. Waves of sorrow joy rippling in sunsets streaming dancing like no other song every footfall shimmers wakes of tears laughing... Unbound joy

spring reeds sway in the canyon winds and sing as they dry sun rise is wrapped in moon's embrace death un shrouds the kiss of day... and when the poet is gone everything is a poem, and when tears spill out you can say it's the sunset... and delicate traceless designs never isolated your heart...there never were any lines that needed to be colored in or out of... Lost ...losing nothing ...this precious jewel of unknowing. Drunk on edgelessness, and it's all you ever had. All you ever were. Splendid brilliant precious emptiness. Like entering a dragons lair the brilliance was overwhelmimg...and you found it was your own infinite beauty shining

and the color blue erases the sky ...and thunder appears to divide the storm ,..memories of things done ...and hopes of things yet to be done appear to create the river of time... and you slip underneath the radar you used to use to find love ...and discover a placeless place beyond need... thunder ocean crashing on rocky shore...fantail spray flying shimmering falling backwards splashing into itself ...and warm seas ever present beneath the tumultuous surface ....bottomless depths unfindable ...edges borders ...lines lost in the battle never needing to be won... back starlit waves cresting below the sea wall...murmurings of ancient tales the sky writes its love songs on my fingertips and I point to the vastness swooning crumpling ...crushed into flowery dreams that wilted as soon as they were born... watery dreams slide into themselves and sail away on edgeless seas precious jewel longing to be found ...once seen cannot be forgotten. Oh! This life! Twisting turning blasting exploding always a single harmony

and the moon and the clouds and the sky are one dancing unseen sun reflected on midnight lake's mirrored gaze and one doesn't lead to another.. no one asked me to dance... pirouetting in ever widening spirals of un-restricted ecstasy... light is never captured ... nothing is contained ....all erupting joyfully magically....ceaseless edgeless flowing laughing crying the wowness never stops.....

and the echoes of hope for tomorrow...slide into the wake of last night's dream. Suspended between the spider webs that used to hold you ...all stickiness gone...burned away as brilliant jewels were found under the ashes of somethingness

Snorting with wild hot breath the stallion's thunderous hooves pierce the very ground it gallops across...starlight glistens feverishly in his mad eyes...and this torrent of words has loosed itself beyond any idea of control and continues like a shiny sparkling stream to carve out shadows from the darkness

Hearing her heartbeat echoing in the rhythm of what is .....she joined in the dance and lost her breath her steps her feet her heart her longing for other for a way out as she slipped into sublime unutterable beauty realizing she had never left It was nothing at all, Yet everything she had always longed for... Truly a center less jewel spinning Shimmering bathed as echoed brilliance empty reflections dancing

106

And the sweep of Dawn alights her heart with unheard songs of glimmering drifting shadows... wind kissed sea dreams filled her heart with an untouchable joy tinged with sadness, and a love that could not be contained as it was no longer hers. Nothing was. Suns and moons and starlight streaming through her as her... Pirouetting leaves and sea-birds gliding within a heartbeat of unutterable majesty vibrant pulsating all encompassing this bursting aliveness that she was. She was the life that breathed her

Somehow seekers believe that this is an impersonal thing. Like an armchair discussion. A trip to a fair, a walk in the park. So many mediators think that it's a slow falling into a state of meditative bliss, or no thought. Some try to get rid of the story but... they are the story, or get rid of the illusion but... they are the illusion. So many try to find the space between thoughts. The 'gap'. Then try to string the imaginary gaps together, But they cannot even find the beginning and end to a thought as there are no separate thoughts. Any trying to do something or nothing will only make the belief in separation, which the seeker is, more painful and seem more substantial

Trying to escape confusion or pain merely perpetuates the illusion that there is a you who can do or not do anything or nothing And meditation is especially harmful as it seems to give you the idea that you can ...for awhile. When the belief in methods is questioned it threatens the seekers very existence. No one wants to hear about how many nights I spent on a bed of nails gripped with unseen terror, the deep deep sorrow, the sudden bouts of impending doom. How my chest hurt and I could barely breathe. As mourning your own death hurts like hell. Worse than you thought you could ever hurt without dying.

Many become seekers to try to escape what they consider bad emotions or thoughts. They try to control or escape them. Maybe find some techniques or self help books, then maybe spiritual approaches. They truly believe that this is possible. To feel better. To have only pleasant thoughts. To become a 'better' person, Life should not have to hurt so much!!!!!

An intellectual approach sounds good1 There are many discussion groups. Maybe you can reason yourself into this... Interrogate yourself. But some may discover that as much as they meditate or interrogate or try to change or avoid thought or emotion It simply doesn't work! Maybe a brief respite From the pain (All the while knowing that it will return). All these techniques are like putting a tiny band aid on a gun shot wound. Your heart keeps bleeding. Awakening isn't an intellectual understanding. It's not a belief or philosophy, Or a set of rules to live by. It's a total ripping and shredding apart of the fabric of you and your life. What you believe to be true about yourself and your world. What you believe you and your world should be like. It is The end of any ideas that there is a you to have a world. All ideas of truth and meaning and meaninglessness. All belief in other better more next...

You are a made up character. You arise in the thought stream as do all imaginary separate things. Never separate from this edgeless non moving flowing we call life.... You cannot do anything or nothing to make this happen. How could a river change the mountain springs or winter snows that form it... I watch so many who must constantly reiterate these tall tales to keep the walls that seemingly separate inside from out from collapsing. If they get a tiny breach in them from one belief falling the walls of fear of unknowing are quickly repaired.

Awakening is knowing that the whole shaboogie is made up. The feeling of inside and outside collapses It is far from pleasant As EVERYTHING must go. All ideas Meaning Truth Love...When these beliefs are seen through there is a palpable feeling of release both physically and psychologically

A belief is a thought word idea concept that somehow feels to have substance or solidity taken to be 'true' or 'real'. Actually beliefs are never really believed, because there is always an intuited feeling a sneaking suspicion deep down that cannot actually be cognized that actually what is going on is impermanent fleeting and has no edges. Consequently with this disparity, All beliefs are accompanied by hope and fear. Hope that it's true (or it's not). And fear that it's not true (or it is). So beliefs are like an imaginary line drawn in mid air. Like a soap bubble, Seemingly dividing pure space into an inside and an outside. This tension can be palpably felt physically and psychologically as the biggest belief of all is the belief in separation. This is felt palpably as a self Inside or separate from what is going on.

As beliefs begin to pop or begin to be disbelieved and known and felt to be untrue there is a feeling of ease or freedom as this process may happen either one by one or in long swathes. The constant tension and feeling of effort of someone doing life stops. The constant feeling that life is happening to a self dissolves. There is a seamless ease that is untouchable and always on when it is known and felt that life is simply happens by itself and there are no separate parts or bits. I prefer evolution as compared to God creation or alien intervention. But I know that it is simply fleeting description and that I am my brain's preferences, And that no words ideas or concepts no thought can ever actually capture or touch what is going on

and she walked the beaches of the great aloneness the waves swirled around her ankles the scent of the sea reflected the sun and moon unstitched upon her brow .....and music streamed out of the home she used to know as she danced footsteps into the wind......

MID WINTER SONGS

And what can you know for sure except this beautiful unknowing?

Unrehearsed the passion play writes itself with rivers of tears, gurgling laughter, love blossoming and empty petals drifting, all into the edgeless ocean where the sun is always rising always setting

There is an obvious zing of unknowable aliveness that seems to recognize itself. Yet not until the moving three d light fabric is broken into separate bits called thought words do things and a knower of them seem to appear. The sensual field is far to vast to capture with streaming thought.

And how could he move his breath so beautifully caressed by this loveliness that reflected untouchable sighs. A love song without time or words or melody, a blazing symphony bursts fourth from within and without from everywhere from no where... from whose Lips whose words whose tears whose love whose shadow lurks inside the deepest darkest secret of night? ...even meaninglessness loses its empty shadow ...the taste of taste flows through me as me like clouds through endless edgeless sky... life tastes its own unimaginable beauty and soars through me bursting into bloom ever petaling wonder singing itself ...Love rains softly through me and sings... Flowing poems thought dreams rippling an untouchable undeniable essence of what has no name nor can be kissed with words... we are the rippling kiss of a poem

Walking as naked as love we are only as close as a whispering dream ...A Constant swoon into and through yourself.. a constant union of what was never apart echoes dissolved in laughter and tears

she spied her empty footsteps dancing through the sky twirling into a daydream as vast as love... she remembered an infinite meandering of unwoven arabesques like clouds dissolving disappearing into their own shadow... Whose hands tapped her on the shoulder and whose love raked her heart across the sky... and whose kiss plunged deep into her being and ripped her apart so the stars could shine so magnificently through her as she was starlight streaming. Where was the key to unlock the rainbow and where was the path to know where? Where was the bottomless chest that was her heart you turn around to face yourself and fall through... and unspeakable joy and wonder fill the gaps where hope and fear used to live... there never was a steady place to rest, a special way to feel or think or act. There never was a person doing something it was all a mirage a play... spectacular... No longer trying to find a place to hang your hat, everywhere falls into nowhere. Everything falls into nothing. Solidity is lost as the knots untie themselves. The sides fall off the empty cup, the bottom falls away... And all the fullness and the emptiness Spill away

reality loops like endless negatives falling into itself and how many tears does it take to keep the sky from crying... the whisper of a dream remembers all you had wanted... this is it. life timelessly streaming in an unbroken peace

Like empty footprints in the sky, Even the longing was never lacking. The day that love died all hope for other dashed. sublime aloneness... When all dreams of other crashed. Yet the waves continued to crash on the shoreless ocean, Falling back into the sea... Sparkling reflections on sandy beaches... Water pouring through water... Light flowing into light... Softness flowing through softness... The hush falls into and through the hush. Emptiness overflows. sliding gliding streaming rushing roaring tumbling gracefully easefully on and as the trembling tip of a wave that had never separated sea from sky

it is the very delicate wetness of our I's that allow us to see the very tenderness of our skin that allows us to touch. The very softness of our hearts that allows us to love. Knowing you are a made up character yet living and loving fully human fully alive. The joy and awe of simply being goes continuous... the knowing feeling of seamless edgeless brilliance embraces the mind with a stillness a seamless ease that is always on... unwritten yet seen, unsung yet heard, un-contained not anywhere nor everywhere as there is no place nor non place... felt deeply never captured nor held this centerless shimmering treasure that you are

and though a thousand suns sink into the ocean the water never boils away. I heard a distant voice beckon from across the water and watched my hands try to scoop up the depths so the song could fill my heart forever and tears fill the depressions where ideas of love once kept me from you

It is a fullness surging and ebbing... can't call it sadness or joy or longing or love or awe. How many letters can you throw into the wind before they have forgotten how to spell? Where do my tears go? There is no template for life. No plan no box to catch it to store it. No way to fix it or break it.

Words twist and twirl and sparkle and shower rainbows in the darkness and lose me loosed unleashed no longer words not mine not yours and dissolving with a sigh a forgotten memory of their flight, like a shooting star that leaves me breathless forgotten in the shadowy depths where there is no place nor time. There is no one to lose or win. There never was a singing shadow locked in starlight's basement.

Life is like a roundabout looking at itself through a rear view funhouse mirror lost in a sidestepping tilt-a-whirl where it can only see itself through its backwards reflection. Lost in your beautiful eyes I catch a glimpse of my own beauty and weep. I can never see myself. Through you I know love

In looking for a secret place to hide a place of rest a place of understanding there are many handholds. Handholds being more and more concepts to fill in the great emptiness you feel inside.. and outside... Yet there is no need to hide when its realized that there was never anyone to hide, nor separate places to hide. It was simply a spinning thought dream that seemed to create a center with a pull towards an inside and outside.. but there was never anything stable or solid that needed to hold on.

awakening is not about becoming a fulfilled self or a better self or a happy or blissful self ...or a non self or a true self or finding your true nature... there is simply no self to become fulfilled or better or happy or blissful or true or false or have or not have a true nature... that supreme infinite empty vast ness that calls you that you fear is true

colorless colors weep as lineless lines fill in wordless silhouettes that sing in dreamtime magic of the wonder of what cannot be yet seems to appear.. and love caresses your loneliness with a supreme aloneness.... like the moon realizing it is utterly alone and everywhere he looks he sees his own reflection tears pouring through you drowning in your own love... achingly heartbreakingly beautifully sublime

Nothing can be done to fill that hole in your heart. There is nothing outside of what's going on. So where would this thing come from/ Aching to stop aching. Trying to stop trying. Desiring to end desire for other better more next. When deep down you know... There is no other better more next. It is a self perpetuating loop that cannot untie itself. Somehow the brain sees through the cage of words and recognizes that all separation is made up. There is no desire to fix the self or others or the world. This shift is uncaused, but it is most often preceded by a personal Armageddon. It hurts like hell. It's not that the self dies But It most certainly feels that way.

and forever trying to balance on the edge of what is and what should be there can be a sudden or gradual release by no one of nothing utterly unplanned or unbidden you collapse into yourself and the fathomless depths of peace reveals itself and love becomes the undercurrent of all there is basking in the sun of utter rest... nothing need be done or undone. The knots untie them selves

and late afternoon sun streams through the windows reflecting on random motes of dust that dance and swirl in un-traceable patterns... just as the sun cannot choose to shine or not or the moon reflect its light or our eyes to see we cannot choose our likes and dislikes or with whom we fall in love it is seamless utterly spontaneous stream a dance without time nor non time

and as every signpost vanished into the mirage, every direction pointed back to where you had never come from nor ever gone... and every time you tried to quench your thirst in the living waters your hunger to fill that vacancy inside ached more and more. More wandering in circles inscribing your name in the sky forgotten forlorn footless you found yourself peering once more into your beautiful reflection aching for a kiss.

and you fell into and through the mirror as the words the directions the plans the maps fell away and suddenly the rocks and waves and bottomless sandy bottom fell through you and into the sky and clouds and mountains above not lost not found the rainbow reflections on the surface were indistinguishable from the shimmering on the bottom and where was up where was down you no longer cared to uncover or hold the gem for it was everywhere and no where it was you it had always been awareness aware of being aware through the centerless jewel of you

Pools of utter delight ripples sing songs of love. Gossamer moonbeams ravaged and shining in love surfing naked in pools of midnight... ripples wrapped in underglow no longer caring to capture the horizon and wrap your dreams inside yourself fearing that they might be lost. All dreams of what life or you should or could be like simply dropped away...

and you feel this utterly obvious marvelous vibrant aliveness and you cannot capture it it has no name nor non-name it has no place nor non-place it is so grand it must be outside of you, you assume you couldn't possibly be this unseen aliveness and this magic this magnificence fills you and pours though you and empties you leaving you breathless... and yet you feel it inside of you too it is always on, looking and feeling like anything at all. It has never been separate from you. You have never been separate from it. There is no inside nor outside nor here and there... this and that me and you is an idea like the horizon. If you cannot capture it you cannot step outside of it there is no outside no edge to what is going on. it is almost unbearably ravishingly beautiful to realize that you are it

Yet only in the dream of separation can we touch and dance like feathered wing tips laughing and weeping in the wind... and echoes of love songs swirl and gather in rocky crevasses where the wind teases out the marrow and blood and sends them twirling down the canyon kissing rushing rivers and dancing in whirlpooled wonder at their own reflection.... We are that jewel that song unsung yet heard in the deepest darkest echoes of our hearts... the utter sublime magnificence of the impermanence the unfigureoutabil-ity the unbearable wonder of life kissing itself though us

life breathes and we appear... songs of infinite beauty and love and wonder in love with the song unheard singing from inside and outside painting flowing dreamscapes of direc-tion and dimension and time. All and Everything and nothing disappear as soon as they seem to arise like an ephemeral first and last kiss of a backwards sideways glance... the dance tripling through its own steps without beginning or ending or middle or goal or rehearsal no ticket needed. You find your dance card empty as the dance floor falls away. Your hand dissolves as you find your self swaying to the music that has always swooned through you as you... a touch a sigh a kiss of starlight lost in the daytime dream of sunsets glowing in your gentle face... love spins and ricochets the dream as the handhold of love looses its shadow. The mind slipped through its own grasp

my hands were clutched so tightly on who I thought I was... my knuckles white, my heart frozen with fear trembling always with not knowing, yet desperately wanting to know. Needing a place to stand to rest to stop this whirlwind of life that I wanted to control.... grasp a piece of it and put it in my pocket, take a photo of the moments I liked and hide the ones I thought were bad hide my head under the covers and scream..."enough!" it shouldn't have to hurt this much to live yet somehow the very storm of desire pried my fingers off myself my hand opened and I found nothing as I dissolved in seamless sky

and there is the weight of your feet on the sand and the light and salt spray and wind kissing your cheek, a symphony of bodily sensation, and thought and feeling rushing swirling, all happening all by itself, all inseparably recognized, how wondrous! and you are the sea and the sand and the wind and the light and the thought and the feeling and, well there you are never lost never found always never this nor that nothing solid nor stable nor fixed

and although it is still dark the birds can sense the dawn their song leaks through my windows ..... and bleeds into my sleep and light floods in the darkness and dark with the light and in every breath of life there is the breath of death and my heart is always broken and love flows freely through me. it is an ocean of coming and going, yet ever remaining stillness. Life is the kiss this of and that falling though each other, never quite written, a watercolor of love painting itself on the river of sighs

I am all the songs of all the lovers of all the poets and songsters of love who ever lived and all those countless unprotected hearts that will come in the future. Like endless ricocheting parentheses extending outward and inward endlessly this centerless jewel that spins so marvelously shimmering innumerable facets of love's heart magic piercing beauty melting frozen hearts that long to bleed into the sea of desire and lose themselves yet fear it deeply. Love is like a necklace of skulls. What would it be like if this song you long for is not yours. What would it be like if this love you long for cannot be contained in your heart. What if it was never yours?

We have become this flowing memory of love singing itself through our lips our kiss our unowned hearts a spinning centerless jewel gleaming through our beautiful I's... infinite facets reflecting bejeweled mirrors dancing in a touch a kiss a sigh an echoed dreamland painting your pirouette in the sky. Knowing we are made up, that love is made up, still I dance as love the lover and the beloved... an ever present swoon into and through everyone I see... so beautifully love sings itself

as a kid I would stay in the pool for hours and hours bobbing up and down, up and down then sink to the bottom of the deep end in total silence and I remember jumping on my bed trying to fly it is like that now weightless, utterly effortless as there is no one left to effort and no one left to be free drowned and yet simultaneously breathing... It all slips into the flowing. It was always Simply Elegantly Softly brushing A butterfly kiss One tear away. Wordless songs pierce your heart and silence blooms singing color and light and wind sails through you as you

Love unowned is like an all en-compassing rainbow where the colors have escaped their lines and fell through you and caught you and you swirled and twirled and could no longer find your face in the mirror and no longer cared

Thought reaches out. To touch. And draws another tendril of emptiness across imaginary space. You can never cross this pathless land as there are no sides... this imaginary reality made of thought dream beliefs and memories swirling into imaginary lines weaving spider webs, never catching the vastness... no poems can catch your tears, yet your hands move methodically through the emptiness drawing endless hearts, stories writing themselves on a sigh on a ripple skipping across this twilight dream where tears flow as a transparent brilliant river sliding into and through a shoreless vast infinite ocean. I slip into the outgoing tide and dissolve into the edgeless sea. The known has fallen away... I see the moonrise over the far horizon as center-less light pours over the silken sea. I look for where I was and find nothing. Everything and nothing arises utterly spontaneously unrehearsed, totally at ease with itself, crystalline clarity burns all things pierces your heart with your very own intensity and swimming in the shoreless ocean our tears are the water of life, and in hugging you I hug myself, the universe wrapping itself in its own inescapable infinite embrace. We are unknowable centerless infinitely faceted gems shining through reflecting each others beautiful light

And crystalline spheres of brilliant light can never see themselves. Your obvious beauty and light is so bright so all encompassing it blinds the seeing of them. You cannot see your own brilliance. We use a mirror to see our beautiful eyes and the universe seems to use our selves to see its own majesty and mystery.

the mind will try to grasp a rainbow and squeeze out the colors... Trying to find another picture that fits its ideas of what color is, yet all letters unravel the words collapse into the vastness where time died. Living in between a kiss and a Song. Breath and colors swirl, Painting a picture of you on the wind

Words collapsed into themselves. They were never written. It was only their essence that sparkled into a jeweled fabric dancing on the waves. Shadowbirds flew across the shimmering, but they were never found. I truly cannot fathom why I ever wanted another moment. To try to fix the sky. There is no concern to where the need to capture to hold the wind the song has gone...the song that sings you that is you holds you embraces you in your own love. Out of the blue love sings like this... words weep through me and paint the emptiness with awe. The knowing always of utter indescribable completeness floods me it stupefies the mind of this and that.
We are songs that sing themselves... alight in the darkness and kiss themselves into being... and fade as soon as you thought you heard them. They vanish into a rippling memory, erasing themselves. In the night without time the flowing is not still nor moving. The fullness the surge the touch of life is you dancing... if you look long and hard and try

to count the stars you may get dizzy. How can you not weep when you never did find the end of a rainbow? How I ran and ran trying to find the edge of the rain. Yet I could no longer tell up from down as I fell into sky skinless starlight poured through me as me and the waves lapped on the edge of a shoreless see

Morning sees itself bloom into day through a windowed glance where lips kissed ancient melodies into a song a breath a sigh falling back through itself... silent yet heard slipping like wind through your fingers caressing your cheek your heart piercing like a saber shattering all your dreams of yesteryear and the morrow... time has lost and no one won

Innumerable stories flow through this mindstream painting an etch a sketch outline of footprints in the wind. How beautifully fleeting this glance of butterfly kisses reflected in moon glow... enamored with their own refection sometimes they drown trying to catch a glimpse of themselves with beating hearts and wings... the scent of lightening rushes through the meadow and long grasses sing your name imprinted in your heart a desire to sing... rich and lush beyond measure a fantastical flowing thought dream colors in your silouette through the prism of your kiss... like a song you long to hear but cannot remember a whisper of a touch that burned kisses into your heart it was only your love that opened your heart

a chorus of winds streams flows through you and sings simply tears reflecting your beauty like ripples in the thought stream bathing in the undeniable wonder of what ever seems to appear

and what can you what could you what should you do or not do to grasp that which cannot be grasped or ungrasped this longing which you feel and somehow has been labeled as wrong... tears..what is life without a seed growing without roots reaching without sun streaming in and through and illuminating the seed pods flying in the winds what is life without hello here I am I love you, you're beautiful? always your own kiss always your own love' always your own reflection shimmering in the evening breeze... yet it was never yours... the passion play paints itself in large wide swaths in delicate footsteps melting in rainbow tears forever and never circling and plunging into you through your heart deeply

untold songs flow written across the pages with tales of unbearable joy and dizzying heights unfathomable depths and deep deep despair and joy and sorrow that cannot be expressed... a show unlike any other moves across the stage basking in footlights shadows dance and sing with incredible sound and color and rage and deep deep kisses and laughter

love and love lost pen your name and a symphony of the worst and the best life can offer plunge and crash through you with un-wavering memories of melodies heard and unheard seen and un-seen watched by everyone and no one... tears unravel endless wet-ness signing the pages of your life

gazing at the backbeat of what had no broken mirrors of countless fruitless dreams gone unheard gone unsung yet unable to be undreamed... this hope of ever more yet seeing feeling death breathing all around you consumes itself in a fire that could not be extin-guished the desire that you were left ashes that blew away in echoes of forgotten foot steps across a vacant street

yet you could not see without your beautiful face, Could not feel without those tears, Now weeping endlessly through the world a broken heart full of ashes the rain of night needing no blanket the Dawn cannot escape an early fabric of bird song, Nor night escape your beautiful death

And where were his dreams that had propped up the canvass that had shielded him from his own brilliance, where he had painted ideas of peace and love? Where were the tides that had contained his madness that drove him to the edge of everything and nothing? Where the vastness sucked out more tears than he believed he had. The vacuum of love had ripped out his innermost being and he could no longer find A border A barrier Anywhere. Simultaneously everywhere And no where Everything and nothing

the silence creeps in when the looking for it stops... it roars drowning out the noise that you believed was yourself... all the endless effort to create peace only made you not notice the peace that was always here. All that chasing after rainbows, Trying trying try-ing so hard! How it hurt to feel incomplete1 Always frantically looking for the missing pieces of the puzzle that you knew had to be there... out there, Kept the feeling of sepa-ration alive... and now life is simply life... love ripens and falls and all of it is sublimely OK. always falling into the mystery and awe the vast edgeless brilliance that simply cannot be captured with words. It's like an ever blooming flower the petals blossom and fall magic reveals itself endlessly All thought emotion sensation all life dancing itself through you as you. Utter ease as you soar through the shoreless ocean of edgeless blue And Always. The setting sun...

and he longed to go to a place where time forgot where endless blue kissed itself where he could lose himself in the shimmering and he could not imagine or find such a place where inside falls though outside and down slides through up where there was no place nor non place. It was his longing for what he knew not that kept him spinning in circles and kept that imaginary center in place. Neither here nor there nor in between... The signs could point nowhere that he'd always and never been... When he lost his feet along this endless circular path only mad dancing remained. And he laughed and he laughed great tears that slip'd him into the sea that had no reason nor non reason. And ripples ran through his brain that tasted loves essence in the moonlight reflection's soundless sonata

without any effort or non effort the sun slides across the sky, and as if by magic it can feel as spontaneous as it truly is and you feel like the wind as the wind blows though you you never had to do a thing in your life you never have... it was never your life

you are a flowing tone poem... Ripping stillness echoed dreamed memories streaming across brilliance unending nor begun you are a streaming dream not the dreamer. You are fleeting flowing description painting itself and dissolving in the flowing... the brush is not in your hands yet tears have rundown the windows and cleaned off the paint

How wondrous that we can wonder at wonder.... that beauty and life and love cannot be captured. Ripples of reflected light sparkle in your lovers eyes.... Echoes in the dream. As silent arpeggios fall on deaf ears as the storms of seas unleashed cry out and ready for nighttime, the sun extends its shadows across the furrowed land reaching for today yet not tomorrow... and the mighty river cuts through the canyon and mountains of earth move toward the sea... sun and moon shine indifferently on the flowing and where are all the thoughts that have streamed through the day, and where are all the tears you've shed?

and where are all the days and nights that have danced through you kissing your shadow into an unfathomable sky-like brilliance... memories swirl like leaves in the wind they fade like mist in the morning sun and when there is no longer any attempt to grasp the sun the warmth and light is overwhelming and we lose ourselves in this sublime clear moonlight illuminating the canyon walls

knowing that life is more wondrous than words can describe yet try to capture it just the same. We can imagine the giggle of a friend's daughter we have never met

His entire life for as long as he could remember his throat had been parched, his heart ached with a thirst so deep it could not be quenched. He was on a continual journey looking for the source of water. He searched the deep canyon rivers. He searched the meandering streams that swam across grassy meadows... He looked in rippling mountain streams, In hidden dark places where the springs gushed forth, In the winter snows, In the summer rains. In the Dragon clouds that sailed through his mind. All leading to a vast shoreless ocean where his heart dropped through oceans of tears. As he realized he had always only seen his own reflection. Through the immeasurable vacancy that could never be filled. Nor emptied

Majestic and precious jewel this crystalline lens that you are... fleeting brilliant window a Reflection seeing it's own reflection... light knowing its own brilliance... the universe touching itself. Singing you

working in the garden sunshine spilling on the plants her hands her fingers... rosemary scent trailing behind her as juniper berries rolled off her hat her breath her movements the sky the sun her heartbeat a seamless timeless streaming without effort and the mind simply gives up trying to make sense of life... time loses all meaning... Meaninglessness looses all meaning... location-less we dance utterly naked without need or goal and vivid luminosity subsumes all and everything dissolving into itself memories lose their grip as inside and outside dissolve into each other and we are lost in unthinking awe wordless wonder supreme bliss

and I walk in moonlight midnight crickets full on now... froggies yet to come and I am all the walkers that have ever walked up this canyon, daylight moonlight or utterly in the dark and my heart breaks constantly as I see others pull their cloaks of beliefs tighter and tighter as they are strangling themselves out of fear of love ...and night hawks swoop and swing through the moonlit night I hear my heartbeat reflected in the clouds. I see my reflection in my lover's eyes, and there is no you nor me... I cannot find any lines... Whose tears ran down these cheeks? Whose feet were dancing? What song flowed though her.....This liquid love

How many mountains of food you have eaten in your life how many rivers of liquids have you drunk how many oceans of tears... How beautifully the dream crochets itself with every word every thought. A dream beyond compare that simply cannot be understood or believed or imagined. This unbearable aliveness that we are

That thirst that you wanted to quench that achy Breaky heart you tried to avoid it is who you are and when there is no longer trying to escape it or run away from it somehow it runs in front of you circles around and kisses you deeply and embraces you and explodes you and implodes you... Into nothing and everything simultaneously... Into every place and placelessness until there is no one to be lost or found And after your kissed from within you are never the same. Simply vast immeasurable spaciousness, empty and full. No space to be filled. No fullness to empty.

As all looking for your lines looking for a source looking to quench your insatiable thirst to know, paints more and more layers of blue on the sky. I am crocheting a woolen blanket and as I crochet it the clothes moths fly out and hit me in the face. Death in life. life in death... And we are the ever blooming ever wilting desert spring

Mirrored shards pierced his heart and ripped the flesh of hope and time. Empty bones scuttled down the sidewalk crushed by relentless footsteps and blew through his shadow... As his Bejeweled crown toppled weeping shimmering wetness bled into the sea... In and out collapsed into themselves slipping through an infinite vaulted chamber where sea fell into sky. Moon plays on echoed tears, Where gulls swoop and call. Shells rush and roar tumbling on sparkling midnight shores The anchor lost no harbor found... Adrift rudderless primordial songs shimmering

Faded tie died memories bleed into the sea. Tattered bits of silvery threads bathed in lost reflections glimmering glowing sinking falling into and through an empty space that can never be filled or emptied

A sideways glance at what you never saw reveals an echoed time space of fairy tale memories a nautilus song

Watercolored dreams lost in morning mist the heap of darkness shattered the circle of shimmering holograms dancing a multi storied castle, wind whipped dissolving into the shoreless sea... Forgotten gems split asunder shimmer as they sink into the inky blackness. Treasures untold as love lost its shadow. Unborn tide's rippling reflections lost in the wake less dream

evening comes to the canyon shadows slide into the reds and bleed into the deepest corners strains of yesteryear float on the winds as they softly caress my cheek, my eyes are open sailing on breezes soaring on waves of awe washing over under and through me as me the web of beliefs that heavy cloak undone naked skinless with nowhere to go there is no one going. Whose storyline floats in the distance as evening bathes the sea of unknowing. Shimmering gossamer threads of nothing. Sparkle in the setting sun. Without love we cannot find our self. our face is lost in fading shadows empty shadows dance and sing in the tall moonlit forest their song is but an echo you heard in last nights dream. their steps describe an empty space where someone used to live... they cannot be captured yet they are felt as a wind against your cheek... a self referential web of nothingness creating phantoms of desire... torrents of rainbows slide down your being as you move softly into the sigh... evening song spills from your lips and slides like deep kisses into your heart. And we are welded melded inseparable... petals drift aimlessly softness permeates unseen essence intoxicates... self is an empty wind an unsung melody leaves dancing

If only I could find a picture to dance this song. There are no words that can capture what has no name, yet words slide through and write our tattered stories transparent threads weaving delicate untraceable tapestries so beautifully as they magnificently self erase

wetness soaks through the words sometimes and bowers of petals swoon into your heart as broken love songs fall through the windy glance of beating vibrating quietude listing in sparkling sees. Every drop a kiss that melts your heart ...flooded broken open and pouring through each other's sun drops of whispering footsteps that cast your imprint in the sky. Streaming rivulets of ocean's tears smiling sunlit dreams. Shimmering like a centerless jewel in your own reflection. We are the streaming dream of separation. Singing itself as ancient cascades of wonder... When we meet our stories merge. Stars swimming through the mind stream illuminate the sheer loveliness where stories of love and love lost bloom in intertwining dreamscapes flowing majestically into the dream of we are. Alighting and playing weaving through her like old lovers kissing secretly forever

And she drowned in the sea of unknowing. Where anchors lost their weight, And there were no ropes to bind her no bottom to land. No harbor to beckon. No sky to promise. No morrow to dream of. No past to wither. No one was left to be saved. Or drown. Or know. Or not know. The sea of dreams washed over her as she lay in sea... the wetness was beyond imagining. The light dancing and playing on the ripples so majestic, She wept and wept, And sang

and sun and shadow chase each other across the mountain cliffs warmth and coolness pulsate on my skin and winds whip through the pines as they sway and sing my friends speak and pause at the beauty I cannot make out the words, I am continually blown away transfixed as un-utterable awe

Thoughts about the past, thoughts about the future all spontaneously arising in this ungraspable momentary. Past is undone no future yet to come, there is truly no place to land, it is all falling. A hush a timeless stream an indivisible flow, a dancing in mid-air with no where to go and no one dancing just this dance and the music comes from everywhere and nowhere

Watching this passion play paint itself with sky on sky... my lines write themselves when I see you, paint me and fill in the color laughing weeping silently singing... Rich and lush beyond measure a bottomless treasure chest... How I thought I wanted only emptiness, but this fullness is sublime

It's like an onion peeling itself. Layer after layer sloughs away... More and more transparent.. And in the end there is not even nothing... Not even emptiness is left....Yet the layers are where the flavor is

simultaneously dancing effortlessly between the richness of the worded world and the vast unknown How wondrous when we meet one another as our stories run through imaginary time crissing and crossing painting shadowy images on echoed canyon walls. Knowing full well that we are castles made of dreams as we feel the wind slide through our transparent being, there is no need to find a place to be... Lightness twirls

and love flows like nectar unobstructedly from this ever blooming flower the petals blossom and fall magic is revealed endlessly and pours out like honey from lips that are not mine. We are tattered love letters scattering kisses in the wind...

How many beautiful stories have painted themselves into my heart how many heart songs are simply woven memories unwinding themselves into the fabric of who I am. I exist only in the touching Knowing that there can never be really touching.
It's so beautiful knowing that we exist only in a touchless touch. Always ending always beginning. Never ending never beginning. The story of you of me of we intertwine until the edglesss glance reveals that there were never separate people to kiss... only a touch a kiss a song seems to paint a reflection of an echo of a flowing sigh a rippling arabesque of me... Sky in sky... Not lost. Not found Kisses itself in the whisper of wind

And as she looked for the source of her tears she found waves of rainbow shimmering dancing in wetness... Hotness sliding down a beautiful pallet of sorrow and joy and love... We are the beauty as it weaves itself. Never done nor undone Reflections shimmer into and through each other Leaving only a sigh stunned by its own reflection weaving itself as life's beautiful impermanence

And layer after layer of gossamer threads dissolve... Hope and fear releasing itself... There was nothing under the cloak of belief. She thought this must be what she had wanted, This emptiness... but there was no celebration until she returned to the land of the living... She stepped lightly out into the dream wearing a diaphanous light gown of wonder.

This made up dream world rich with separate things tastes sounds colors galore castles built of illusion where love and beauty dance with death will come crashing down. That is truly beautiful1 No one wants an unfeeling frozen hearted life gripped with fear. Yet some seem to find their walls plastered with fear. No light penetrates

and smiles turned into birds rising in the morning sun their wings shone with reflected light echoing loves dream in their beating hearts as they soared lost in loves gaze... you are, we are love is. How amazing to be amazed at our own amazement. To know that we know

and our stories write themselves like a songbird enveloped in music wonder abounds without the canyon walls the music could not resound and echo so magnificently shimmering reds and pinks in reflected light we need our feet to dance and lips to kiss and voices to sing... awe spreads the wings of my heart I weep endless rainbow tears that flood the sea of dreams where I emerge drenched in my own love. All I can do is wrap my endless poems around this tear stained world

He tried to find before and after as ships sank quietly in the night. He turned around hoping to see the sunrise and Found himself adrift On an empty sea. He heard his echo calling his name and lost his reflection in the clouds

Unrehearsed the passion play writes itself with rivers of tears gurgling laughter love blossoming and empty petals drifting all into the ocean where the sun is always rising always setting. Swallowed spit out everything lost in nothing. No longer preferring emptiness she danced beautifully gracefully seamlessly balanced between love songs written on a heartbeat and death... As the wind blew through her and wrote songs of fleeting caresses and fiery dances that burst into flames and ashes lifted and swirled into spirals that wrote meaningless poems across the sky

I see everyone as naked awareness gazing out through a veil of tears. It's like my heart is always weeping. How could I find myself without this sublime ache? What I longed to lose has become the most beautiful precious treasure

As soon as you are born you cry out. The passion of the universe unfolds... we are life's longing. How wonderful is that? Now it's simply about sharing our beautiful humanness. That's all that's left. life as a human being is filled with great sorrow and unutterable joy and it will break your heart

silent steps upon darkness fall as shadows gather where sunlight stops only the echo of memories fills in the spaces where you once lived and flowers are so beautiful because they wilt... And as you cried out wanting to hold onto the magic of life your fingers combing the vastness.. Searching for a hand hold, a place to rest. Somewhere safe... somewhere to land. As the last bit of hope for other better more unties itself... tendrils of emptiness unweaving a bower a dream of gossamer thought. The last threads of feeling like a separate observer. One who does not change. One who will not die. Some kinda essence. Something unties the moon and its reflection sails through you...

Reflections of scattered light shards dance through the shadows of streaming afternoon sun across the carpet reveal an ancient text that crumbles as it is written. Lost words sing of places remembered and forgotten pierce deeply. Exposed and raw the point of this and that loses its edges on the banks of the Delta, slips through your empty hands as the dream slips into the sea.

Your tattered petticoats flutter in the final eddies and whirlpools before the brilliant sea of vast light swallows the remaining remnants of tomorrow. You lose your skin and it never grows back. Just a transparent naked shadow shimmering in love's reflection where you used to be.

Tear drops fall into reflections of yesteryear and erase themselves in oceans of joy. The flood of sorrow falls down empty cheeks and slides into transparent jewels dissolving into their own wetness. The treasure unleashed was never hidden. It was your very brilliance that lit up the sky and illuminated the universe.

There is no escape from this majesty as there is no one left to escape. Just as the echo of afternoon rains sparkle on the street as their reflections blow seamless sky into smithereens of color. Remnants of clouds slide across the mosaic of your heart. This unbroken nature of nothing folding into itself all things emerge and simultaneously disappear. There is no concern as to where they have gone, or what will come as there is no behind or forward in this melody of one.

Your tears shimmer and sparkle in the last rays of sun and dry in the winds that brought you here that you have always been... So beautiful... So marvelous that we can weep at our own unfathomable beauty

We are magnificent imaginary unique holograms, stories that write themselves with gestures of light flowing through light, swirling flash cards creating an illusion of solidity, that immediately erase themselves. Using air and breath and fingers and symbols to sing love songs across an imaginary divide... astounding

dawn greets the setting moon birdsong floats through the window. I stretch my toes into the daytime dream and perception floods my mind. Thoughts appear and I begin as the morning sings this indivisible seamless flowing. Is utterly un-caused, it cannot be grasped or captured in any way for the one who would hold it is part of the flowing. Mind cannot grasp itself. Life is super complete in and of itself of itself, so nothing can be added to or taken away from this un-compounded symphony it is truly a miracle that anything seems to appear at all

swallows swoop and swirl high upon the canyon cliffs. I am standing as I soar ease fully as them. Stillness dancing... all sense of personal volition gone long ago the universe streaming through me as me. Dancing through the ebb and flow of tides and love, yet not separate from it. Winds blow through me and songs of fleeting sparkle and shadow caress and dance bursting into flames... ashes lift and swirl into spirals that write meaningless poems across the vacant sky

He caught her shyly glimpsing his painted rainbows as they dissolved into tattered remnants of prayer flags rippling in the wind... Where was the solidity she had hoped to capture with her butterfly kisses that unraveled as they almost touched. Her hands moved methodically through the sand trying to find something to grasp. But the waves revealed her nakedness. Forgotten bits of shells no longer carried the song of the ocean. They tore off her abandoned petticoats as every idea of solidity, Of certitude, Of truth, Of self, Of other, Of love, Was shredded. She found herself clothed in tattered ribbons. A necklace of skulls swinging madly. No ticket needed for this dance. No rehearsal. No dance floor. No feet. No wings were needed to soar, just a backbeat of empty shadows swooning through their own light

needing nothing but an empty song to say I love you, Sails unfurling endlessly bathed in sunsets glow... Moon kissing your toes as your rippling reflection dances in a vacancy, a dearth of song sings itself... And I bask as love's memories rushing into the swing of day...

oceans of tears wash the make up from the looking glass as the words slide off and you fall through... every shard ripping you to shreds every secret dream unraveled, until there is no place left to hide and no one left who can... your heart ripped inside out all that love you were afraid to give for fear that you would lose it pours out and you realize that it was never yours... this sublime skinless touch... his heart song needed no fingers to pluck the strings

and the silence sang as light crashed though the darkness in timeless rhythms that danced through the mind stream never capturing what he felt so deeply. Yet like a net thrown into a river every crossing of the lines held innumerable jewels of his own reflection. Sparkling shimmering memories like filigreed curtains catching the light as it passes through... never held nor grasped the stories paint themselves on a river of moonlight ... a deep penetrating current that is your song yet has no words and is all words where joy and sorrow merge in a timeless symphony echoing loves delight at its own magnificence

mirrored glances falling though each other reverberating ricocheting like endless parentheses as his hand moved through the blueness there was no solidity merely echoed dreamscapes singing sky like vastness... explosions of emptiness create after images on the mind screen that dance and swirl to all the songs that have ever been written and have yet to be written... insubstantial with no inherent meaning or purpose, ghostly dancers mirror their own dance... beautifully surreal this dance of this and that... the wondrousness of no things and all things..... like an explosion of love of peace untraceable magnificence

In my daytime dream I am the wind as it blows through me, I am love as it flows through me. I live between everything and nothing. An assumption a wisp of gossamer dream imagined into a vastness. Without wings. Skinless as through indescribable softness. Bathing in the edgless waters of my own love. When my head hits the pillow its all flowing. words cease. And I wake up and stretch my toes into the world of things... Dancing on the edge of everything and nothing... It's like I blink my eyes and the miracle continues

And suddenly we see, it's as if the scales have fallen off our eyes, this most wondrous world that has been here all along with no division or split anywhere... a seamless timeless flow utterly without meaning totally ungraspable and most marvelously we are no longer separate lonely isolated individuals... yet there are no others

The trapdoor opens and there is no ground to stand on and no handholds to grasp and no hands with which to grasp the emptiness... no symbols by which we can grasp this seamlessness, and there is a beautiful quiet and softness when there are no edges, nothing can ever be cut the sharpness the edges are gone, they never were. Sides fall away bottom falls out and even nothingness spills into the vastness. Meaningless ness and meaning dissolve. All this and that is seen to be a superficial overlay. A thin miraculous iridescent sparkle on the waves. A shimmering dance... and the only place we exist. Sailing on your own tears sliding into the sunset. Slipping through the stream of nothing we see glimmering lights of memories illuminating the whorls and swirls with rainbow reflections of who we were. We find ourselves turned utterly inside out.

like ripples flowing over ripples radiating in all directions and simultaneously flowing back over and under and through themselves rainbows reflecting upon each other love swallows itself only through this unique prism of self can the rainbows be seen or love or beauty or the natural perfection of life itself. You are this infinitely multifaceted centerless precious gem more rich than the music played by every musical instrument ever conceived or yet to be... the rush of life can never be captured but the mind reveals the colors and tones and magnificent variation plucking harmony and form out of emptiness. Creating silence and music

winds paint the air with memories unsung brushstrokes fly softy on wings of untold dreams, and the picture is so stunning you lose yourself in the dancing... magic twists stories out of empty skies as they fly away on seamless wakes that cannot be followed

You are a tender musical reed effortlessly singing the song of the universe and simultaneously the universe sings you as you are the wind that plays it... this seamless dancing ineffable yet vividly apparent wild naked free un-contained, unutterably perfect precious jewel... this crystalline lens creating the wonder the magic of life... the flowing the dancing the unitary soaring of life of in as and through itself

roads are dipped in sadness and my feet sail on wings of joy and they fly together through the space of nothingness of silence singing the path laid out forever... turned in upon itself into the vastness and back again walking alone in sublime union through forests of after images traced upon an endless blue sky... and sun and shade dance upon the canyon walls and echoes of emptiness call my name they twirl and twist around as silent laughter resounds brightly, how easily light and life flow when there are no obstructions... clouds slide effortlessly across the canyon skies tracing unfindable moments that leak from the day through your heart and through your veins... the universe sings your song with wordless words striking chords of emptiness into this symphony of perception

Life spontaneously lives itself without beginning or ending yet it is always beginning and ending. There is no place or time yet it includes place and time. You are everywhere and nowhere, everything and nothing simultaneously. There are no things or non things to change or move or be unchanging or permanent.

Silence sings, emptiness overflows, as life kisses itself through your lips. As you are the portal through which love and beauty enter the universe.

I see your immeasurable beauty beyond what you think you are and just as you think you are, your emptiness and your fullness, and am astounded. You cannot see your delicate tender eyes, but I can. You can never see your own magnificence, but I can. Only through each other can we catch a glimpse of our overwhelmingly unutterable beauty. Only through imaginary separation is there love. The precious jewel you've been looking for is you

Oh! The thrill of simply being, utterly naked you have lost your center and your edges, you are vibrantly alive, your heartbeat is everyone's heartbeat your breath is the same breath felt by everyone who has ever existed... your thoughts are not your own as they rise and sparkle out of nothingness just as all perception and instantaneously disappear, like stars shooting across the inky blackness. how magnificent! This life happening utterly spontaneously without effort or non effort no one needing to make it happen every indivisible moment totally complete, nothing can be added or taken away from this singularity it is all encompassing fully whole without edges. un contained. un-bidden. un-contrived. un-rehearsed Life does itself without rhyme or reason, and knowing that we know is marvelous the gem of the universe awareness aware of being aware through the streaming dream of you

And all the starlight sucked into itself dry as a bone, an empty shadow danced in utter darkness until he saw the tender ache of his own reflection
Weeping

All we can ever know is this illusion
yet somehow some brains can know that this named universe composed of separate things and events is an illusion, a magnificent infinitely patterned mirage made of separate colors and hue and richly varied timbre and rhythm that appears to dance and weave itself through our eyes......

and where thought and imagination cannot go .... where you cannot go ......a sublime
edgelessness where description ends.....
it is marvelous breathtaking
...you go so far and there is no one to sing to...
a little farther
and there is no one to sing...

so we turn around and notice this unreal reality as if for the first time
where it's always like your first and last kiss
every one you meet is your lover

the awe and unspeakable peace subsuming all and everything simply blows you away
Yet you find your feet
...so you can dance
You find your breath
....so you can sing
You find your lips
.....so you can kiss
You find yourself again
.........so you can cry and laugh
And love

it is like you return to a house where you used to live, and it is utterly empty. all the
windows are broken and the doors and shutters are hanging by a rusty nail banging in
the wind. there is dust and empty dreams, dried leaves and memories and spider webs
blowing around in circles in empty corners. Yet, you need a place to live. you need your
imaginary lines to touch. you need that set of old clothes left by your empty shadow to
dance. so you move back in, yet the walls and roof have become transparent. no longer
clouded by personal intent or hope and fear of love of life of death

we live beautifully suspended between who we never were and nothing at all. Homeless
we are always at home. We are nothing but empty memories. footless, we wear these
shoes to dance. line less, we are these stories that write themselves. and we return to sing
of what can never be kissed with words

And the bejeweled enchantment that you are that I am dances as an infinitely mirrored
dreamscape of castles and dragons and fairy tale kisses in the dark and deep deep
secrets that seem to reveal themselves as they tell our tales. Like whirling gypsy skirts

flashing hints of color twirling and form dissolving and reappearing and flowers laughing breathing a spell of unutterable beauty with you in the center, it's all an unspeakable soundless symphony painting time as colors slide down the window creating curtains of light and sound and pictures of who you never were. For under that mask of tears there was never anyone to feel joy or sorrow or feel that song well up in your chest or feel that caress from the inside out of your heart song breathing.

It has always been a magic carpet ride of tapestries woven and un woven with infinite threads of nothing and everything as they twine into shadow and light dancing across an unfathomable unknowable silence that cannot move or shimmer without your reflection.

Without your beautiful beautiful magical eyes there is no color or form or trees shimmering in the moonlight like a fairy dance in a clearing that you couldn't quite catch except with a sideways glance... The dance begins anew yet it had never truly begun nor ended.

As we are kaleidoscope bits of colored thread revealing the song of separation strewn like stars across the vault of sky without meaning or non meaning... until the apparent distant suns are written into a play with romance and war and birth and death. And love. Yes love, that jewel that gem that garment of wonder that sublime mystery that speaks in every language but can never be caught with a word or symbol or thought or idea, yet love is an idea as we are simply most marvelously ideas.

an imaginary flowing dream made of colored bits of memories flowing in a whirlpool of thought that seems to have a center. But it is all without a baseline, a river. an ocean to flow to. Time is an ocean of nothing and flows without hope or fear as it echoes in the empty streets. Primordial song beckons your heart beat from whence it came where it dissolves... Waltzing a two step showering kisses across ancient tunes of yesteryear... memories gleaming shimmering shadows singing... love met and lost itself in the brilliant hush before worded forests hid the dance... always beckoning you to join but you could not as you were stricken with fear... Fear was your name it was your badge it was your shadow it colored all and everything with a bitter brittle flavor. How did love melt your fear that defined you that held you from light pouring endlessly through you? Your tears may tell a story as they lie in pools of empty pathways gathering dust dreams aglow in moon song.. you have traced your backwards glances and found that they are empty as the morrow's sigh

What I sing of I know you recognize. You know this deep deep deep in your heart in secret places that thought cannot touch, that what I sing of is true beyond any ideas of truth or lies. I hear your songs of longing and I recognize them, they are truly beautiful. I know without a doubt that you are truly beautiful, just as you think you are.

It is impossible to believe or understand but somewhere deep inside you know that everything is perfect just as it seems to appear. That it couldn't be any other way, because if it could then it would be that way, wouldn't it?

Perhaps you have been longing for someone to tell you that you are perfect. I know without a doubt that you are, and that your longing is perfect. For life doesn't happen as it is supposed to, or as it is meant to, it simply happens all by itself. Just as suns rise, wind blows, rain falls, hearts break and tears fall. Time may seem slow or fast and sometimes it feels like it stops. So much of life is happening without your thinking about it. Walking, breathing, reaching for a glass of water, loving. You never ever planed who we were going to fall in love with, did you? You probably never ever planned for life to look like this... for those parents those kids that sickness that death... certainly there is no conductor or controller of life.

It is truly beautiful how thought tells the story of you of me of we of twirling down the canyon, of autumn colors shimmering, of weeping at the beauty of moonlight upon your lovers face, of birth and death and sorrows and smiles through that under mutter that constant stream of words in your skull. It has to be perfect, doesn't it? No one is doing it, you are certainly not doing it. In fact without that chit chat inside your skull there is no you nor skull. You are a miraculous dream, a story, a magician's tale that tells itself, paints itself in the wet caverns of your brain.

Deep deep deep in your heart you know this magic but you cannot have it. You keep twirling around because you feel that maybe you can see it from a sideways glance. But you can never see it there is no you to see it and yet seeing happens, never separate or apart from what is being seen. It is beyond logic or reasoning or understanding or belief, but there is a reason you have been seeking a way out of the dream there is a reason you've been seeking oneness for wholeness for completion which is not a thing but something you vaguely remember. That is why imaginary separation hurts so much! It simply feels wrong! But it can't be wrong you can't be wrong nothing can be wrong there are no things. It's all perfect, believing in the dream or not believing in the dream, and no one chooses one or the other. As both are the dream, there are not two ways of looking or seeing there is only seeing and the seen inseparable as a symphony silently singing the dream of you, of life, of love, the dream needing two to kiss, to dance, to sing to itself.

Just.
Like.
This.

I love everyone's stories. Like mine they twist and twirl and dance through the emptiness without trails in shadowy glens where the morning mist evaporates in our beautiful love light.... when I know I exist only as this story and that it is made up,,, a magician's tale... there is no concern or need of the morrow.... yet I love love and bask in your beautiful warmth and light.... knowing you are simply another trail of tears swimming in this sea of dreams...one foot in the dream the other soaring as vastness
your heart always naked and unafraid... as the wind blows through you and you are the wind.... dancing

....and walking in wonder stardust glimmers in my forgotten footsteps....

.......creating shadows of nothingness from imaginary tales....
....and the moon seems more luminous in my skirt of dancing shadows..... yet ripples of starlight cascade through the illusory spaces where love flows..,
....I need a space suit and gossamer wings to play in the dream....
....and this rainbow cloak seems to create this character of a dancing girl... they stream through my being and pull my hair from side to side....
...and a starlit blanket wraps around me and I am starlight itself.....
....lost forever as emptiness and found again in the storybook of love.....

One by one or all it once the knots untie themselves revealing a brilliant infinite even expanse without any effort or non effort, without anything needing to be done. As all trying or trying to not try are the knots tying themselves.

Love's glorious display enlivens the timeless now with the grace of magnificent indivisibility.

Searing pure light burns away all imaginary shadows of this and that. There is no possibility of going back to believing there are individual "things"--thoughts, emotions, sensations, moments --that have an independent nature.

All is the seamless love expanse of open unbound perfection. We dwell in perpetual ease and discover that we have never left this blissful all encompassing expanse. Pure uncontrived ease and wonder saturate every moment.

There are no limits no borders, no center, no corners or inside or outside. Nothing to hang onto as there is no one to grasp and no things to hang onto. Simply love shining as nothing less than everything.

This ecstatic love dance is super-saturated with even-ness and equalness without any reference points whatsoever. There is a Joyful stability no matter what seems to appear.

Swooning in love as love through love
No longer confined to ideas of twoness or meaning or non meaning or freedom or non freedom
Or anyone to be free or loved.

LATE WINTER SONGS

and she ran... breathless into the rain longing to feel alive to let a lifetime of sorrow dissolve... to feel inside and out merge... she watched her footsteps melt into the pavement as every tear drop reflected in pools of streetlights... colors drenching her ideas of freedom or bondage of wrong and right of here and there of this and that... as a water color picture of who she used to be streamed down the empty streets... kissed by her own demise she faded into yesterday's flowers and watched her shadow dancing with itself

And where did time begin ...if not when her story started to write itself across the sky... she looked and she could not find a wake..... splashes drifted rainbow clouds across her path and she was mesmerized ...hypnotized by her own reflection. Cast adrift her shadow longed to find its source. Sometimes she got so dizzy and exhausted...yet she longed to give up to lose that mantle of imaginary control

It was as if she was suspended between the rainbows glittering on the surface of an edgeless ocean...and their rippling reflections on the vacant white sands below. She could no longer tell which way was up. Or down. Often would get terrified and retreat to a shore of belief where she sought rest Until one day... she could no longer pretend the shore was safe as she noticed the waves were crashing on her... She drowned in oceans of tears... Saltiness merged with saltiness... Reverberating reflections ripple across and through each other...and she no longer cast her dreams into the sea... looking for reward they had been dashed on the rocks of her own demise. It is like she was one half of a kiss. Longing to fill that hole in her heart. Yet that aching loneliness morphed into sublime aloneness... A constant union her heart overflows...with what she was trying to grasp... Hugged from the inside and the out the sides disappear...melting into and through herself

Closer than your very breath... than the tongue in your mouth... releasing the words that have never been yours.... Slipping through you ....as you are like a vessel that has been turned inside out... Your heart overflows...with what you feared yet longed for...Pouring flooding rushing roaring emptiness overflows

Your tears never left a trace as your story wrote itself across the sky..... You have always been dancing as this timeless rhythm of this unowned symphony. You were merely a reflection like seeing a face in the clouds. The moons gentle kiss upon the water. The ocean glowed in shadows smile. Your life becomes waves of unowned memories flicker-ing like an old movie projector on the ocean night as empty shadows blow across the edgeless sea. When you spied your reflection across the horizon songs beat madly in unowned hearts Singing themselves. Just Like this

Words like love songs painting a picture in sky stirred by unknown winds and tides like forgotten piles of leaves gathered in corners of old houses ...memories and old dreams and fears about the way things are...and how we wanted them to be just like time is an idea .....the paintings have no real meaning yet they move you deeply like a vibra-tion a touch that penetrates you pierces you in places you cannot find and didn't know existed ...and you find yourself appearing and disappearing like an actor on the stage where you placed all your bets...a tiny part that plays itself although it was never written or rehearsed

The longing to become whole and complete simply slays you your heart drops and the desire is seen to be who you are.... and there is no more looking you were just a picture projected onto the clouds a fleeting path of a bird you never saw a shadow a dance of swirling memories hopes and fears and the attempt to become a real person to escape time trying to define your lines drew an imaginary silhouette

and now the battle is over as you breathe deep the sun that was always here..... and the winds blow through you... As you only in the thought stream could they play like dolphins in the shimmering reflections rippling they could see each other... laughing ....weeping... drowning ... existing only in the shared dream of separation... without thought they sim-ply were each other... and knowing and feeling that Swooning through the swoon

silently singing of the vastness of the beauty and magnificence of this tender fleeting-ness of the shimmering ...and love bathed always in the orangey reds of sunset there is a sublime bittersweetness knowing that the closer we get we simply disappear

your hand comes up empty as you try to catch the sky your skin cannot remember the feel of the evening breeze... like looking at moonbeams through a directionless lens reflecting you back into yourself. Sparkles of dancing light on rippling seas like fireflies disappearing and reappearing... and oh! the transience the immeasurable beauty of this tender heart wrenching life... pain and sorrow break you wide open... and you are it and it is you

All a flowing emptiness... spilling rushing streaming as it does all by itself. Nothing can be sifted out of it or added. You stretch out your hands and the universe pulls you into the vastness. You find your own tears ...fingertips touching your own wetness. The winter wind spun autumn's leaf... It's palm loosened a memory of a kiss, and a breath of love swooned into itself. Your shoes were never laced. The clasps never clamped you to the ground. You tried in vain to hold onto the earth as it was spinning. So afraid you would fall off into space, yet thrilled at the idea of falling. Endlessly. Neither up nor down

Where did the fear go as it left your desperate grasping hand. As it faded like early morning mist in the summer sun? That clutching at your chest your heart beating wild. You were the fear itself. The fruitless attempt to steal the air ....like a bandit unmasked you wept

And the evening sang itself. The touch of a midsummer love song, an imperceptible caress a butterfly kiss fell through the moonlight dancing on the tip of her tongue. She fell into an endless sigh. Moon rise swallowed the shadowed guest as wind blown dreams crashed in echoed star light

his footsteps his hands his heart were empty yet trails of blood belied a fantasy of castled wonder... a place to rest had not been found all the musical chairs had been removed. One by one the banquet had become a memory. The food spoiled. Until the tablecloth was pulled out, the cloth an idea of what the night would bring, and what daylight should sing

Weeping at the gust of sighs wake less ripples captured his reflection. Shimmering in evening's delight Beauty paints itself. One day you peer into the mirror of another's eyes and recognize them as your own. And all ideas of beauty crash in wonderment... the whispering of golden jewels no longer haunts you. No more grasping with a hollow tongue this utter all encompassing ease of seamless being can never be kissed with words,,, yet words are part of it... and like sunlight and wind seem to play in the autumn leaves yearning to dance yellow into magic lanterns... and like the horse seems to ache to gallop across the empty meadow ....and like winters empty branches seem to elegantly reach into the heavens yearning for spring rains... and like the first shoots of crocus and daffodil seem to push through the softening dirt aching for a taste of sun... and like cold mountain winds rush and roar down the canyon seeming to ache for that hot dusty desert so they can undo their fury... and like deep deep rivers seem to ache for the sea

and like the sun slides across the vault of sky and seems to ache to kiss the sea, bathing it in its delight of yellowy oranges and reds... awareness aware of itself though its own shimmering reflection seems to enjoy the dance the swing the song long summer grasses pierced with early morning sun dripping with crystalline dew... lanterns singing tales of sunset waving rippling golden pouring into deep silent greens.... And she saw infinite hue and timbre contrapuntal dancing swirling twirling sweeping kissing merging from palest yellows to the deepest blues

.and oh! The play of shine and shadow this tinsel sparking on the tips and edges sliding into deep unfathomable rich heart piercing darkness..... dancing waving folding weaving unweaving bejeweled wonder........ the richness the fullness of infinite color and taste singing itself a mighty wind blows through her ...is her she is the dance the enchantment the life surging and urging the suck and flow of this waving magnificence! All her footsteps were unwoven in the sands where time could no longer hold her.... Skinless raw and brilliant beingness was all she had ever wished for yet it was nothing at all. Yet love finds its way to draw imaginary lines across and through the edgless vastness, and we live in between the push and suck of timeless tides

and he lay beneath the ocean of fear and longed to fall into the light above. Crushed he could not move. His heart ached for freedom his hands tingled to get wet his shoulders ached to sob. His wings to soar. He tried to loosen the rains that bound him but the trying merely tightened the knot. The ache that defined him. He could he not see that he was powerless. To cry or not cry. To wish for freedom or not wish for freedom. To long for light and love or not long for love. To see clearly that he had no power. That there was nothing he could not could not do. All that waving never sends those prayers to an empty heaven. Sky is always beautiful yet does not know it... wind sails down the canyon and smiles like ripples flowing across fields of grasses never lost never found yet vividly apparent

like the reflection of a kiss on an edgeless sea no lips can be touched... shadows dancing lost in a field of dreams like a song you cannot quite recall, yet the words are always on your lips and where is the space between the taste of a tear and the ocean that swallowed you whole?

The edge of the cliff enchanted and terrified her. The sunset was so beautiful. So tantalizing. Like a moth inexorably drawn to a flame. Longing to fall and simultaneously longing to be held. Terrified of losing herself. Yet there was no her to lose. There never was. She was a dream a fiction an assumption a magicians tale. Fleeting description dancing weaving a story of a life of love of sorrow of deep kisses and laughter stories that magically weave themselves into a lightgown woven with sorrow and joy walking the dark windy rainy streets A wet umbrella under my arm. The gleaming pavement in the headlights and the heartland of home has never been lost. The sigh never leaves. All pervading penetrating underlying all and everything melting... into your own caress... inside and outside dissolved into each other this vibration this pulsating aliveness of this and that The heartbeat of existence allowing awareness to be aware of itself and every note arching with innumerable overtones.... creating a symphony... silence and a hush a breath that sings...music of unbearable beauty,,, you have become wonder itself... beauty looks in the mirror and weeps

ahhhh.... slipping into and through each other... lost in the imaginary places inbetween... love is sublime its like watching your lines form as the passion play sings and unsings itself being the character and watching it and knowing feeling that it is a dream and all your friends and lovers and that old man down the street are made up... and love and madness continue... yet it is known they are also made up,,, waltzing pirouetting dancing themselves into a world of separate things and ....time.. a river a flowing where your tears can never be numbered or caught or signed ....and the sun could not see her infinite beauty but everywhere she gazed she saw her own intimate Infinite reflection

and when the lines are known and felt to be imaginary an unknowable beauty overwhelmingly naked and unadorned... reveals itself,,, there is a direct intimate honesty as you no longer feel separate from what is going on.. the made up world of things becomes unbelievably immeasurably wondrous the imaginary line between inside and out disappears tears ... such unnameable beauty and what she could no longer name she felt surging through her as her

it is uncontained unrehearsed uncaused ... you reach out your hands and the sky pulls you in... you stretch your toes and the bottomless depths swallow you...and after you are consumed by the blueness you are forever part sky ....it is the nakedness the rawness of life unowned...unhidden...not lost nor findable....... the dance where twoness slides into itself hearts touching falling dissolving... like this

she saw her own reflection and the music sang itself ..waves formed and crashed onto the edges of a shoreless ocean...and finding touching weeping into their own wetness dissolved into the sea slipping sliding dancing in as the flow .. bathed in sunsets dream and unknowing cannot be spoken of it is a sublime unknowing when there is no one left to know without doubt or confusion or non confusion word sing themselves and sing us into a painted flowing water color picture bleeding into a dream ...a river called time is needed for our tears to flood into and the rippling creates an ever emerging momentary that catches the sunlight

and rocks and rolls and trickles and streams and dances and twirls into circles of whirl-pooling shadows that eddy and flow into and through themselves we are simply tone poems blossoming and falling aching for the light to strum our colors into streaming lanterns for just. a . brief . moment. a window a touch a breath a sigh a moonbeam fell through her open door and wept on her doorstep sobbing infinite colors and hues and uncountable inseparable oceans of light spilling flooding tasting touching aching for the taste of taste where life saw it self and was delighted and amazed at its own wonderment and sang and dove and slipped back into the flowing... back into the hush... back into the softness... that it always had been

Words jump out of the inky blackness and rainbows write symphonies across the sky that spill into your heart and dash against the sea leaving traceless rainbow reflections in your eyes arabesques in the sky left by the heron's wing ...traceless sighs slip into the flow-ing.... beauty revealed . never caught...

like ripples flowing across fields of grasses never lost never found yet vividly apparent like the reflection of a kiss on an edgeless sea no lips can be touched shadows dancing lost in a field of dreams found only in their rippling reflection and I have become the song I ached for and always seemed to miss yet I could not quite recall the words they were always on my lips..... the taste of taste the warm liquidity the ever present flowing of home naked unadorned direct intimate closer than close inside out life and you are Soaring through rainbows where once you tried to fly your kite of hopes and dreams

you were an imaginary self looking for an idea a shadow looking for its shadow and the mind wonders why it had seemed so hard to find ...nothing

swimming as pristine emptiness...fullness pours a warm bath of edgeless love. When I speak of this.... lines and edges seem to appear only to slip back into the flowing... Featherless canyons flood your heartbeat to softly touch to creep to crawl to find that which is unfindable. The desire to dance is the dance

And the hush stills the longing to end the longing There is an endless sigh that flows in rainbow colors..... an inbreath that sings you..... a kiss from the inside that impales you a song that sighs you without warp or woof yet woven with butterfly iridescence dis-solved as the notes are sung. Infinitely blended into a contrapuntal atemporal symphony.

Where color light and feeling merge into a deep current of untraceable unfindable kisses painted by moon reflection

He could never lose himself. Yet he could not find A Line Between the inside and the outside of this wondrous kiss where time lost its footfalls. Only an empty beach danced in the colorless surf of midnight and waves of sorrow crash into waves of joy and sparkle on empty beaches of a sea that has no shore

Its like a touch ...a kiss....a breath a sigh ....gently wraps around your heart..... And washes you out of yourself. a caress of emptiness Spills you Into And Through yourself... all the pieces of your life fall apart and tears rain like colored dreams down an imaginary wall between you and life... the wall disappears as you fall through. You no longer look for beginnings Or endings Or why You wanted to kiss your own hungry lips

Clouds stream shadowed kisses through billowing light dreams rippling shine and shadow into images of this and that Creating caressing land and see and shadows cast by nothing dance... grasses ripple as wind's song... silence echoes and falls through its own reflection

a sigh pours through a sigh. A hush falls through itself... day slips into night... the dance of time... reflections echo through silent shimmering iridescence and flowing shadows slide through ripples on a moonlit ocean waves crashing blood roaring silence steps on the the empty streets perfect symphonies never written.... love songs un-found yet sung trying to see to touch to feel to know the magic simply kept you a breath away

and she asked what is going on? Searching the sky in vain the wind sang her name and caressed her cheeks and the sun warmed her tenderness and slid across the vault of sky and blueness echoed her wonder and clouds were enveloped in the orangy reds as the sun longed to kiss the sea she began to ache for this very fleetingness that she had oh so feared... and suddenly she knew yet could not sing of an edgelessness so vast she could not grasp it... of a deep deep knowing beyond dimension or non dimension... or meaning or non meaning and there were no more questions as the one who would ask had dissolv'd into the wind's whispering song

self is the effort the grasping the trying to catch the jewel the magic the life you feel is rushing by when the efforting stops it is like a runaway train hitting a brick wall ...all that momentum propelled by hope and fear of a next that never existed is over as you fall into and through your own hush... suddenly there is no one doing life no one to whom life is happening... simply not even nothing or everything... your heart cracks and breaks and is shattered into a gazillion pieces and drops and you realize it was never yours... all the scaffolding falls away crumbles as the waves crash into themselves you fall off the imaginary timeline between birth and death and the overwhelming hush disappears into the singing of singing

Starlight flowed through her. Windswept beaches sang her name. Even love flowed into the vastness of uncatchable awe. Her fingerprints like raindrops on a river that Sank into the night sky. Whirling around trying to catch her shadow created a circle which she could not untangle. A centerless circle untied itself

She stood in the doorway of her own shadow's dream and fell through a place that had no time. Deep in sorrows joy she found a mirror'd glance into places unfound. They told a tale where her whispers swirled. Inside and outside flow into and through each other and all ideas of more or better or effort and achievement fly out the window. Sweetness reveals itself as you. The path you walked danced sang along in starlight's sungaze dissolves once again into the great unknowable vastness

She could not find where her shadow kissed the sky.....what did blueness taste like ..... and she sank into a sky puddle and tasted indescribable love. Her glittering shoes were abandoned on the sidewalk and the streetlights heard their laughter and her tender breath was like the essence of ever blooming flowers dropping countless petals that soften a frozen reflection. How the colors swirl disappearing as your rainbow fingers touch a glance where you once stood looking for yourself

she tried to count the stars so she could lay them on her pillow at night and dream of other worlds where stars need not be counted. She tried to capture a moment a feeling a thought a rainbow to hold to capture to point to the dance neither camera nor paintbrush nor word nor finger could point as the pointing become the dance ....the crown starts to slip and the jewels slipped into the flowing as she stopped trying to hold them... she realized that there was nothing under the crown... the radiant empty shimmering was everywhere and no where... how playfully shadows dance and sway pirouetting into sun words ...like crystal spheres illuminated by moonlight dissolve at daybreak

songs like painted photographs point to the rush of an immediacy without time. She flipped through old moonbeams searching for a kiss she had lost... whirl pooling water lilies streaming a deep deep current caught the petals swirling dancing reflections transfixed with their own spinning tides where colors laughed as they bled into the dream the magic was the slipping through her hands It was the fleetingness that was so beautiful... fear and hope dissolved revealing her nakedness opening like a flower planted in the dark kissing sunlight streaming through her heart every heart ...unfound yet never lost the reaching for beauty was the beauty...the longing to dance was the dance....the ache to merge with the flow was the flow...it had always been yet never was

and the wind rushed through the empty rooms and she found herself weeping as she stepped into her new light gown... dancing. She sung in contrapuntal resonance after the hush had slipped through her breath. The strange and beautifully familiar tune that sings when time truly dies. Every layer ripped off of a light so bright it shines right through you. Revealing the majesty of what was always here. That song On the tip of your tongue. Waiting to taste itself. You are an untraceable love poem writing itself...images dance and swirl like shadows of last nights moon on the tip of a thundering wave that you cannot see

As you were reaching for the gold ring somehow you fell off the horse and found yourself in a vast edgeless meadow. Rippling as summer grasses do. Listening to the heartbeat of the universe. We are the current and the ripples laughing dancing in the sun as it pulls us along simultaneously. The hush inbetween the breath and the song. The lips and the kiss. It cannot be found. Yet it is always on

And no one could tell exactly when she danced into the sunset. She was the wind and the sea and the colored raindrops like tears sliding over their umbrellas. She disappeared into the whispering winds and returned to feel their breath their kiss upon her lips

He no longer needed to fix the clouds just right as the rain fell through him. Bejeweled webs woven of moonbeams starlight echos sung as the brilliance un loosed from the weave... ebb and flow of life's unraveling... Traces of unwritten songs heard on your fingertips.... Lost in magic. And the unfathomably quiescent ocean... Disolv'd into yourself the blissful liquidity of home

Strings of melodies floating ,,,my feet gently padding. The kiss of twilight fades in the darkness. A soft quiet envelopes you hugs you from the inside out. The hush falls through the hush when neediness fades. A lush all rightness fills the air and an essence of indescribable beauty that has no edges or knives the empty richness of life unowned

Patterned arabesques slip and flow and dive through bejeweled pirouettes of streaming sound and unstoppable colors merging submerging twisting turning falling through rippling dreamlike unfound sighs where ease rains sparkling effervescence kissing sideways glances felt wholly deeply a magical show with out beginning or ending, yet always beginning and ending. Fullness beyond measure roars and rushes through glittering transparent emptiness as it enfolds you embraces you carries you soars you without measure or rhythm.... the inside has exploded imploded through the inside and no edges can be found. There are no words to capture this infinite fluidity, beyond freedom or containment Unstoppable yet unmoving grand and magnificent without time or place. Swirling dancing into a dream of this of you and me just like this

it takes a bit of getting used to there being nothing here...life flowing through you as you... no solidity... no place from which to jump... or stand... or fly... as there is always soaring the ease is constant and untouchable... no matter the storm or calm above all pervading wide eyed awe.......... like the weight and softness and light of the ocean,,, the enormity of mindblowing vastness... reflecting in every ripple ...an utterly obvious stillness,,, shimmering ....Fingers moving colors flowing no space no rhythm or rhyme or place it needs to be held... Love flows like sea weeds wave in the shallow warm seas

You are the breath and the song that sings itself. The meterless patternless patterns that dance footless on an imaginary stage in the footlights glow. You are the wind and the tree tops dancing. The sunlight playing shine and shadow on the sidewalk. You are the imaginary space between no spaces. The light and the shimmering reflections waltzing on the waves. The ebb and flow of sea and clouds soaring in sky and day sliding into night, and this heartbeat of this and that...of up and down and inside and out There can arise a deep all pervading untouchable peace when the illusion of inside and outside collapse into and through each other

When the circle is complete there are no more ends It is like an unending first and last kiss

Your footsteps leave no trace there is no past nor path to nowhere. What was the day where was the hour of first of last of few of many footsteps echoing on the empty dance floor? Where were the clouds what was sky when it hid in the Suns pocket?

love a beautiful dream of here and there and you and me buckets full buckets empty yet the pouring away of the sounds of laughter of sobbing rippled in wake less waters... memories kissed a dance into being and he sighed as an immense toppling of dreams of castles in the air of seashell'd mirrors crumbling into sand... Where was the vessel you had tried to save in you heart after your song had ripped all the scrolls and texts and musical scores and notes and melodies and overwhelmingly beautiful kisses that sang in the night?

starlight passed through him as he bathed in his own reflection never and always had lost their bearings in this unbearable beauty that lacked nothing... this hum of pure brilliance could not be missed as he hung his clothes in the winds of moonlight

Self is constantly looking for more beliefs to strengthen the wall of fear of unknowing, as it is constantly being ripped ...the wall is glued together with hope and fear as no belief is really quite believed. Sometimes that wall can get a rather large chink falling out of it... and there can be a glimpse of the vast unknowable beyond. Most scurry to fill in the blanks with more ideas about the vastness, And some step out naked into the flowing... Weeping and laughing subsumed as awe

and memories echoes of ancient dreams spiraling in the darkness never inscribing their name in the sky...chills and thrills up your spine laughing at the stars as they swallow you in your very own kiss... Diamond ripples across sky puddles winds singing primordial songs of unrelenting vastness in palm trees shimmering..... tingling aliveness in all the senses tears running behind sunglassed eyeballs... and he holds up a mango and tells of its beauty... and the mango the space his hand all seamlessly falling .....ecstatic wonderment dancing in delightful arabesques of shine and shadow streaming........

To know that the gossamer brush dipped in colored tears paints your story on the flowing ....You are not the painter your hands are empty .....and you reach out to touch the shimmering and your hands dissolve ...and the emptiness overflows into the vastness. Whirling dancing sliding flowing down rainbows whooshing up and catapulting into brilliant unknowingness... velvet sublime sadness has ripped you into shreds... tears flooding oceans depths dissolving into colored dreams gazing dissolving into themselves with sparkling eyes of love. Life a flowing embrace from the inside and out. Such magnificent sweetness of a broken heart and love remembered. There is a sublime deep deep current of un named emotion bittersweet life flows through you as you

Awe and tears and the sea rushing shells swirling seagulls crying. Memories remain after the shift .....yet they have no grip no pull... swirling whirling dancing weaving a story constantly unravelling creating a shimmering iridescent sphere around an empty center Everywhere fell into nowhere As Life swallowed itself. She became the song of the ocean ricocheting through the heavens. Wind and light blew through her pure deliciousness adrift on silent seas of wondrous delight. A diaphanous softness like the essence of seabird shadows streamed through her and caressed her innermost being and swished against her utter nakedness as she soared skinless in a warm summers breeze

and midnight feathered moths fly in endless streaming moonlight in whip- like spirals their flight cannot describe the darkness all effort to capture to know what can never be grasped...falls away....your hand relaxes and you lose your grip on nothing.... and all the lines fall into spaciousness gently as love into sublime unknowingness. Knowing in the conventional sense is like capturing, boxing in what cannot be stopped or grasped in any way. When the lines become transparent and all sense of lack disappears then it feels like love. Pure and simple.

You are the morning song that awakens you. Kisses you into lips and eyes and dancing shadows in the hush that sings you. Shimmering sparkling as the dew on the grasses. Drops of moonlight fading in the sun. Light and dark pulsate and vibrate the rhythm of the night bursts into bloom. Infinite hue and color echoing a symphony of all that you are dancing you caressing your tenderness into limitess fullness exploding imploding supreme brilliant vastness undoes the curtains and says, Good morning I love you. I am you.

rivers swallow'd the seas as they fell into sky. Pure unstained spaciousness vast beyond measure. The enormity the weight the utter lightness of light Lures you... you find you are the tigers breath ...a primordial song of destruction... of all and everything and nothing at all. Erasing dark and light and shadowy glimpses in the night. And unutterable brilliance pours through you as you Burnt offerings blow away... And a shadow bird arises from memories flame dancing

and winds flow though winds and wetness pours though wetness and light falls though light and echos stream through echos and reflections shimmer through reflections and emptiness glows with emptiness and shadows dance into and through themselves and tears glisten with salty wetness

and wonderment pours though bedazzelment and enchantment falls through magic not lost not found not forgotten not remembered no meaning nor non meaning no purpose nor non purpose ....and I find tears drying on my cheeks and remember, Oh yes, Here I am

Swooning into the surf ....your feet... swept asunder... Soaring through the vastness.... alighting falling through stardust..... through your own kisses... caressed from the inside out iridescent wings lit from within the slightest breeze swirls you yet there is utter stillness within the dance... the symphony of perception rolls over you through you as you..... Rolling tumbling streaming falling as the wave itself.... Skinless ..... melting into the oceanic warmth of profound peace... dancing on a feathered glance as your hand reaches out the air the space the apparent emptiness itself cradles and holds your hand... welcome to the universe

and stars sing you as you dance in midnights breeze... your perfect garment surrounds and caresses your beauty... soft steps make no waves as you are held...within and without your own embrace .... your footprints are luminescent fires sending love light sparkles into the vastness touching your lips with tenderness. You find nothing other than this centerless flowing .... softly dancing melting merging burning brightly raging effortlessly .... you are indeed not an outline or an inline or even interconnected......there is nothing other ever than this dance... and this symphony magnificent beyond measure ....tender butterfly kisses softly raging supreme beauty that can never be caught....

You asked yourself to dance and you accepted.... and you turn into you and greet the dawn and blend into the vastness that has always been here. Swirling spiraling outwards crashing into yourself in infinite waves of delight.... Merging back into the warm edgeless liquid sea that you have always been and untraceable edges leave no mark no stain no cut nothing can be found... And daisy chains wove themselves into her hair And sun and moon and stars and light unimaginably naked poured through her as her

..and one day she noticed that the scaffolds she used to hold up the sky were not needed.........

There is a common misconception that enlightenment happens to the person, and somehow this imaginary character becomes a no self. Obviously anyone who thinks that they are enlightened also believes that there was a path or method that they used to get there or to attain that...Where there's nothing to attain and no one to get it. People long to escape their humanness.

As you grow up you learn morals you learn what to be like how to act in society these morals generally coming from some religion originating from some God or giant authority keep the society together

And one of the first ones they try to teach you how to try to be selfless. So they tell you to give some of your candy to Marianne. And Marianne is happy to get it and your parents or caregivers are happy that you've done it and so you feel good. This seemingly selfless act actually was very selfish wasn't it?

So the goal of many of these religions and societies is to become a selfless person. That sounds good to so many because they can't stand this pain that they feel, the loneliness they feel inside. They have been taught that anger and jealousy are bad so they are trying to have only nice happy thoughts and nice happy emotions and act selflessly, but this simply cannot be done. It is quite understandable that some people would be trying to erase or change thought and emotion in order to feel better. However I do not think that unless someone has heard of it they would be trying to get rid of the self.

So there are people who claim they have reached this rarefied atmosphere. Often they are revered and people imitate their actions and speech. They give instructions on how to reach this unreachable place. Seekers love this stuff because it gives them a path and it solidifies the believe in self, which they are. The belief in separation is never challenged. The teachers may say things like do nothing or rest as awareness. All perpetuating the most painful illusion of separation of a doer and something to attain. Doing nothing is doing something. All trying or trying to not try perpetuate the illusion of someone who is trying.
How can you rest as awareness? Awareness is always bright and unhindered .....spontaneously indivisibly awareness and perception arise and simultaneously self release without time or non time Without any effort or non effort.

As these people are revered and given a lot of flattery it often goes to their head. The authority hierarchy power driven cult is born.

I knew one woman who said that there's nothing that you can do or not do a few years later she was giving instructions. Many tell people to drop the story obviously not realizing that there is no one who can do or not do anything and that they exist only as a story. Many seem have just to settled into a self-help program. Awakening is realizing there never was a self or mountain. No one to have or lose a self. Yet realizing that this dream of you and me and we is the only place we exist. And love. And beauty. And wonder. It's simultaneously dream like and realer than real. More vibrant and lush when there is no hope or fear or need of a non existent next. It never feels like there is someone doing life or that life is happening to a someone

There is a constant search to piece back together what was never apart looking for a place of rest called understanding. Trying to make the world make sense. Looking for a purpose or meaning.....

And so many hear my words and they say they resonate with the words and yet they can't get it. They feel there is a missing piece and continue to look for the missing piece in words thoughts.... everywhere they can they are searching for something that does not exist. What they are longing for is the brain to make sense of it and it just simply cannot make sense of it. As it's not an it nor a non-it.....

I know what it feels like the frustration trying to get this, And I can feel your mind spinning in there..... what could be so simple that it cannot be grasped.... What has no edges nor center nor any reference points whatsoever. What is infinite beyond measure without time space or dimension. What is not a what

What I sing of cannot be known in the conventional sense. Conventional knowing is about things and there are no things. Yet it is so mind boggling obvious once this is recognized. ....no amount of trying to get this or capture this or hold this will make it obvious. It already is it is so obvious you cannot see it. But you can feel it. This is it happening right now. Your bum resting on the chair your fingers sliding over the keyboard your breath the sunlight slanting through the window your eyes sliding over the words that you are reading right now... this is always it and you have always been this. It includes all and everything as there is no outside. It is merely the description the story the passion play writing and erasing itself that seems to obscure it, But actually without the story there would be no awareness aware of being aware. As it requires imaginary separation

The story that writes itself with shared learned words seems to separate awareness and perception it seems to separate a you separate and apart from everything that's going on..... Yet there has never been any thing separate..... It's quite obvious that when the under mutter stops for just a brief moment, All thingness and you disappear ...That should tell you something!

all there is is an indivisible spontaneous spacious edgeless vast unknowable brilliant expanse......... pure stainless immeasurable beyond belief or understanding or imagination like vast unending sky pure space infinite emptiness without emptiness thought cannot catch it all and everything…….. all this and that all self arising and self releasing upon inception never having any substantial independent existence no things either moving or non moving like a hologram it cannot be held or captured like a castle in the sky you cannot move in like a reflection in a mirror you cannot seize it… any attempt to escape this virtual reality of this and that or capture it or insight about it is it

as this web of imaginary things spins itself arising and self releasing simultaneously in an ever emerging ever disappearing non capturable unthinkable atemporal instance leaving no trace like the flight path of a bird in the sky

and you who try to capture it or understand it are simply part of the indivisible fabric drawn with invisible ink on not even nothing ….it does itself the singularity and the virtual reality simultaneously indivisibly …perfectly

and no matter how many feathers you sew into your costume you will never get off the ground bejeweled tapestries write your name in the sky… precious gems reflect your brilliance in the stars winds of unknown origin whip your breath and heat your blood into a dance of pure desire for what you know not ancient rhythms part the curtains of your brain and magically the dance steps are known beautiful rivers of thought sliding over and through the edgeless dream highlighting the emptiness with light and shadow… every unique snowflake reflecting the suns brilliance melting in the heat of its own desire…. there is no future and there is no now and there is no you who can step outside of this seamless timeless streaming and manipulate it in any way the wind blows itself

purply clouds sail through edgless greys in evenings breeze… laughter echoing in broken canyons where i once lived …a seagull cries one last time before he rests…and dancing beauty rains moonlight upon this breathless timeless vastness… and the flowing the fleeting the unheard backbeat of the river becomes so loud you melt into its embrace and every drop sings with its own indefinable sweetness

howling for the moon I ricocheted off its reflection and melted into the sun….consumed by my own desire to flee my own essence my shadow turned around and swallowed me… and echoes of laughter ….petals of sunshine rose with the new dawn of heart piercing uncapturable beauty dancing on the first spark of brilliance arising in the inky blackness

the utter undeniable feeling of pure vast brilliant spaciousness …the marvelous supreme transparency… the recognition of uncapturable beauty… the superb ephemeral dance with no edges or sides... or place to include you or exclude you or any forms or shapes or colors... thoughts and feelings and moments merge into the dance... no key is required no ticket is needed to decipher the patternless patterns... the rhythmless rhythms... as as soon as an imaginary reference point appears the swirling seems to revolve around it... around you... and a back beat a heart beat of this and that begins to sing the song the story of you... and me... and love... and wondrousness beyond measure... knowing full well that all time and dimensionality and causality and feeling knowing deeply that all separation is an illusion... the pure unleashed uncontained vastness is always present... and the story a beautiful iridescence swirling over what is and what can never be known or touched but sensed deeply

marvelously the waltz the tango the dance begins... and it is you and you are it and the soaring flowing utter ease sears through all ideas of this and that... And you are simultaneously the hush of brilliant supreme spaciousness and the dance singing itself

Before awakening you feel like you are a person who walks down a street with eyes and hands and feet and a heart and fingers that comprise a body that moves..... and there is a you who has a name and who has a life and that you were born and you are traveling a path sometimes scary sometimes lovely path towards your inevitable death

And you pass trees with leaves and fences and hills and birds flying and you point to a bird and your hand like all things is surrounded by space... And on this timeline you can remember past moments that happened to you and you can imagine more moments when you will do things..... And sometimes you feel like you have a handle on all this and you are doing well Other times you feel like you are being battered about like a ping pong ball Like life is happening to you And you struggle to gain the upper hand...... It is a life of hope and fear

After the shift the lines that seemed to separate this and that hands feet trees and sky..... are known and truly FELT to be imaginary

There is no doubt and no place for it to arise that this is what you have been longing for your entire life and yet it is nothing at all. This unicity was always the case always on, Simply not recognized. There is no need of confirmation or approval. There is no concern for what others may think or believe about what it's like for you. It is known that it cannot be taught or learned or given away. A sage lives beautifully balanced between the edgeless sublime vast brilliant emptiness and the wondrous worded world ...emptiness overflowing ...

Where were the portals to loves eternity
Where was the sky light in his dreams
Where was the touch of midnight in his song

Beautifully never done nor undone
Weaving and unweaving itself an ever emerging wave always the first and last kiss

She pirouetted in silent reflection and mirrors sang of her beautiful dance
Without a dance floor
The footlights dimmed
Just missed
Yet not lost
Memories lost their grip
In laughters sublime sorrow

like a melody you longed to remember this creeps in when you least expect it
when it feels like you've given up trying to get it
...like a summer's breeze caresses your skin
....like a river flows naturally to the ocean
.....Like the sun rises
.......like tears
.........like laughter
and yet not like anything at all
you cannot try to stop trying as you cannot stop the wind
life flows utterly uncontained
it is self creating
utterly unrehearsed it paints itself
As your ears hear and your eyes see and thoughts and emotions miraculously appear
This dancing this soaring this falling this tumbling this sailing this rush! of this uncapturable life

And it may happen that you find your hands have unfolded their tightness
And your heart has lost its chambered walls
And the winds are soaring through you
Skinless tears clothe your naked wonder

Filigree of ancient times lie beneath the waves of sorrow
bursting into waves of joy merging without need of tomorrow

...early in the morning I write in the dark with pen and paper and when I awaken later the lines have run together...

and my words can add nothing yet they sing of love so sweetly
falling through a timeless ease the colored dreamscape dance in awe's reflection

Often wordless wonder pervades and surges into waves that crest on borrowed tears
Gathering darkening clouds of sunshine
And burst into song
Dancing as the tree tops in the winds
As sunshine bursts from echoed slumber casting ripples across the midnight sea
wakeless rhymeless empty shadows dance in mirrored halls where no stones were cast
No dyes were needed to color a dreamscape of patternless vastness

Midnight leaves a bittersweet ache of home

and every inseparable moment a song alighting on my lips
no invitation to the dance is reqired as there is not even nothing outside of this dance

as the dream circles around unfound tales of love and darkness and soars through naked sky

She was a silent symphony a tone poem flowing rushing roaring streaming soaring falling softness into softness
A hush unlike any other fell through itself and silence sang
Rippling as a brilliant
shoreless ocean shimmering sweetly poignantly basking in echoed reflections of loves heart magic

Simply a shimmering all encompassing gossamer light fabric with out end or beginning
a flowing dream of canyon winds and an unmistakable vibrant aliveness
Turning tales of falling leaves whisked into an autumn song
Bedecked in sunset
A smile
A heart
A chorus
Of one

Ahhhhhhhhhhhhh
How can a sigh touch the silence

Even plastic flowers fade
Shhhhhhhhhhhh, she whispered
There never was a mountain
Without you there are no cherries or blossoms or trees or sunlight falling softly on your beautiful face

Never solid songs unsung pirouette as ancient dreamscapes swirl in whirlpools of wonder reflecting only the morning dew

Nightbird shadow slides across a shimmering sea
rippling your lips into a kiss of wonder

A skinless touch between here and there teased sunshine into sailing ships across endless blue

Words like Tattered lanterns
never catching wind or light
Yet foggy skies speak of the magic of wind caressed tears

Never dried always dancing
How could you sing of this magnificence if your heart did not bleed

And roaring thunder breathes a sigh of what cannot be sung but sings
Wordless lips kiss a mirrored sideways glance
The heaviness of braided space cascading ripples of shimmered dreams
A hint of what had no source arose as baseless unfettered jewelry embroidered songs slide into a beckoning dance swirling in a hollowed eve

It was love that remembered him and gave him feet to dance
And urged his heart to gather moonbeams into a shadow once again

He could feel it shining just beyond the ridge of midnight
Hidden still
Yet the essence of loveliness unmistakably free
The taste of light glimmered and trembled into this footless dance

And grabbed his steps
It was simply a heartbeat from here to there

Singing breathing a kiss of words that bloomed into petaled sunlight
Ricocheting in infinite rainbow'd tears

Slipping into forgotten water colored songs
A painting of smiles wandering the desert dream

A mirage unequaled bursting springlike wonder with every footfall

And the only words he could find were I love you

Crocheting his song
blue into blue
Of vast
unending sky

All abounding ease of no edges
Cricket songs fade as robins awaken

Morning tea steaming curling drifting to kiss the morning light barely beckoning through
the window
Canyon walls hide the sun but the first rays peer onto the far walls illuminating cotton-
woods dancing
A slow waltz of shade and shimmering that sing of wind and water and drops of delight

we are like overtones
reverberating echoed dreams of love songs not yet sung

this utter perfection .....this unnamable beauty that fills us and empties us simultane-
ously ......rushes through us as we are hollow reeds that sing ....

.....filled with swirling memories and barely remembered melodies that reverberate to our
own empty echoes that dance freely in vast limitless skies painted with rainbow hues that
cannot be captured yet our tears fall in colored dew drops that sparkle our love songs
across the universe
.....the only home we know....where we cry and laugh and love and live and sing

and oh! ....how your tears are so beautiful... shimmering reflections of love without design
gently kissing rainbow delight
soaring streaming though the vastness no longer mistaken for another song as there is
none
words simply touching piercing you deeply as there are no places left untouched
filling you and simultaneously emptying you until only the hush of a kiss ripples in the air

Baseless centerless echoes
Lost dreams shimmering
In loves reflection
Skinless soaring sky

rolling silent thunder
Gathering primordial sunclouds
sing I love you
bathing in primordial skinless awe

you are never not home
embraced in your own loving arms

METHODS AND PRACTICES

For All Seekers

The belief in methods is the same as belief in separation, in self. It is the same as belief in personal volition. So when the belief in methods is questioned it threatens the seekers very existence.

The belief in a method or practice, or that awakening can be taught or learned or given away is the same as belief in separation, in other better more or next.

These are all ideas like peace or oneness or stillness or any goal that lies in an imaginary future which has never ever ever arrived.

The seeker is defined by the seeking, and if it is seen clearly like a bonk on the head that there is no next, and that without seeking the seeker would disappear, there can arise a great fear.

As without a next there is nothing to do and no one to do it. All ideas of this and that and cause and effect become irrelevant.

Quite simply the belief in a path practice or method is the belief in separation. As that is what the self is, seekers will defend this at all costs.

I often ask seekers if they have ever found an other better more or next and they answer no, yet keep seeking. That is why it is a belief!

Inquiry does not lead to the shift. Nothing does.

ALL trying or trying to not try merely perpetuates the painful illusion of something to get and someone to get it.

The reason seekers get so mad when you say there is nothing that they can or cannot do to get this, and that there is no path to awakening, no method or practice, and really get miffed when they feel we are putting down their teachers or method is because it strikes hard at the core belief of who they are.

The belief they are a separate entity with personal volition, that there is something or somewhere other better more or next.

That there is something they can do to reach a place of rest, of knowing, of certitude, or of understanding.

Awakening quite simply cannot be taught or learned or transmitted.

I am not trying to convince you of this as awakening is not a belief or understanding. It's not about getting rid of beliefs through any sort of process. You are beliefs. You cannot erase yourself. Emptiness cannot be pointed to. There are no two.
How could I give you nothing? Where would you put it?

There is no path to nowhere. There is nothing an imaginary character can or cannot do in order for this to happen, as it does not happen to the imaginary character.
It is a shift that occurs in the brain. You and all imaginary thingness are created by the brain. You are a streaming thought dream. That would be like a deep river trying to change the rains and mountain springs that formed it, or a ball that has been thrown trying to change the hand that tossed it.

If it seems like I am putting your favorite teachers down, well, I am not saying they should not be doing this as they are Choice less holograms as am I. I am not saying you should not be following them. I am saying that there is no you to do or not do anything or nothing.

A sage is confined to the dream just as a seeker is. Yet I hear your screams as you try to escape your beautiful humanness, to escape the only world you can ever know, to expand your consciousness etc. To realize that you are some thing not human, like time-less awareness or a true self, or pure consciousness. Trying to reach some imaginary place. Some mountain top with rarefied air.

I sing, There is no better more other or next.

This is it coyote!

It should be self evident that anyone who charges money for a satsang knows that if you pay money you are expecting to get something.

No one can give you anything, no one can give you nothing. There is no path to nowhere. You will never ever get this, no one ever does.

No one in the history of mankind has ever been enlightened.

There's nothing to get. No prize to attain. You will never get there from here as there is no here nor there nor you to go anywhere or no where.

Anyone who believes that there is a method or a practice that leads to awakening still believes in the dream of separation, still believes that there is a separate person who can or cannot do something and still believes that there are separate moments.

Other better more or next, like cause and effect cause and effect, is made up, just like you.

The objectifying brain creates a virtual reality of this and that, of tress and rainbows and love. some of these made up things refer to things physical like trees and bodies, some of these names refer to things totally imagined like gods and selves.
These ever swirling thoughts of future, memories and the ongoing description of perception of sight sound touch bodily sensation, paints a story of what is going on appears. A pseudo reality, magical really, and in the center of all these thoughts there seems to appear a center.

A thinker of thought, a feeler of feeling, a toucher a see-er a listener, and this imaginary center feels separate. It never feels quite right, and for some made up characters it feels downright hideous, so these people we call seekers search for a way out of the pain and this becomes their life story.

They may hear of oneness or wholeness and that sounds good, so they try all kinds of things to join together all these separate pieces like trying to glue together that which was never apart. All trying merely perpetuates the illusion of someone trying, and it hurts.

It's like chasing your tale or trying to patch the sky together after the lightening seems to separate it into shards.

Some of these techniques seem to work as they give a glimpse of a peace that the seeker longs for.

Perhaps he feels like he is disappearing for just an instant, as when thought ceases for just a brief moment you and all thingness disappear. Yet until Thought returns there is no knowing of this thought free state.

When he returns he just believes that he is doing something wrong and tries harder.

The techniques that seem to work and that give a temporary relief to the pain actually perpetuate the illusion of separation.

ah ha! the person cries! I have done something that works! eureka! I am a doer. The circle simply keeps on spinning spinning tightening the noose and there are millions perhaps who are meditating constantly.
Looking for that peace, longing to make it go continuous, looking for wholeness.

Seeking, basically to stop looking, desiring to end desire, seeking to stop the endless search, longing to let go, yet longing to be held. For if the seeking stops, the seeker disappears.

The seeker Is the dream of other better more next, and ya know, everyone knows deep down in the very pit of their being, that there is no other better more next, and no one to go there for if there were no next... What would you do? What could you do?

You have a glimpse of this feeling of life doing itself this edgless centerless flow and you will do anything to try to get it back.

Yet all trying nearly perpetuates the most painful illusion of separation.

All of life always occurs all by itself There are not a bunch of separate things that are inter-connected. There are no things nor non things. This unicity although it really has no name or non-name is always on. It is intuited and cannot be captured with words or known in a conventional sense because it is beyond belief imagination or understanding.

It's not an it nor a non it.

Although there may seem to be techniques in order that you may feel this, all that these techniques do is perpetuate the illusion that there is a you who has done something or can do something for this to happen. Yet as unicity is always on it need not be contrived and cannot be brought about a new.

This recognition this deep knowing feeling tone of seamlessness can go continuous. There is a seamless ease that embraces the mind, and the most wondrous sense of awe. But you as an imaginary piece of sky you can do nothing for the brain to recognize that there have never been any pieces of blue.

You are that desire you are the clinging that attempt to grasp the magic and you cannot let go.

Self is the grasping creating the illusion of someone clutching and something to be grasped.

The idea that there is truth or an ultimate reality that can be known or that there is someone to know it is simply an idea, or that there is a special place to rest, or that there are any things whatsoever or any reference points.

It can be known in the deepest sense not conventionally and felt always that all separation is made up, and this simply cannot be spoken of as every word seems to divide up this seamless edgeless vast expanse.

You are the dream not the dreamer. This is it coyote. The only world you can ever know.

All that can happen is there is an awakening to the made up mentally fabricated nature of this pseudo-reality. We use the word dream or dreamlike or a magicians tale or pseudo-reality or virtual reality. But really it has no name or non-name.
Yet dream seems to be about the closest that many of us come to describing the knowing feeling that all separation is made up.

It is an unfindable untouchable un-pinpoint-able edgeless vast expanse ever emerging never done nor undone seamless fleeting momentary without time nor non time neither moving nor non moving.

This has no name nor non-name, it is indescribable yet felt deeply. There is no knower without perception. There are no two. Not one not two not none.

All we can know is that there is an un-interrupted indivisible symphony of what we call perception and the inseparable simultaneous recognition of it. This is known and felt deeply. This pulsating aliveness vibrantly appearing as anything at all.

As there are no separate things nor separate moments nor separate observer nor separate thing called life, you indeed are it. You are simply and most magnificently awareness aware that it is aware through this symphony of perception this streaming dream of you of me of we.

Only with this objectifying brain can there be this imaginary twoness. Where never and forever crash into each other. Where meaning and meaninglessness dissolve into and through each other. Where inside and outside stream through each other and disappear.

Thinglessness is simply inconceivable unutterable, and most marvelous.

Here, thinglessness happened all of a swoosh, but it subtly felt like it had happened to a me.

I think this is where most teachers are. Still believing in a holder of things and so they feel they have arrived somewhere or attained something as I did, and they teach methods and practices.

There is a book called the end of your world by a teacher who doesn't seem to know that it is the end of everything and nothing, the end of everything you have held to be true about yourself and your world including ideas of truth. Or that there is someone to have a world.

(I think other teachers have had glimpses and are trying desperately to get it back, and so recommend the practices they believe led to the glimpses).

It took two more years here for all the last beliefs to crumble until there was not even nothing left, the holder of things was seen to be utterly imaginary. I didn't even know it was happening but I did notice beliefs and self judgement and self correction sliding away.

It is known without a doubt that this cannot be learned or taught or given away, that awakening is utterly uncaused.

Self is any belief that there is a something stable and unchanging versus a world 'Out there', which is filled with changing separate things.

Even an idea of a true self or timeless awareness or pure consciousness is still belief in separation, and the belief in separation is painful

But you as an imaginary character cannot do nor not do anything or nothing to get rid of it as you are it.

In the end there is no need or confirmation and little concern for what others believe or think about this shift as it is undeniably present always.

There is no doubt and no place to for it to arise that this is what you have been seeking your entire life, and yet it is nothing at all

love,

Nancy

Made in the USA
Lexington, KY
18 August 2017